BURGER LAB

Daniel Wilson

hardie grant books

TABLE OF CONTENTS

·······	THE ELEMENTS	8
-------	CLASSIC BURGERS	34
———	OTHER BURGERS	56
— — —	ON THE SIDE	96
═══	ALL THE OTHER BITS	112

10 BU BUNS

12 BT BUTTER

20 KM KETCHUP & MUSTARD

22 CH CHEESE

26 CI CHIPS

28 PK PICKLES

30 SL THE SALAD BITS

32 OT THE OTHER BITS

48 FC FRIED CHICKEN BURGER

50 TO ORGANIC TOFU BURGER

52 EB HOW TO EAT A BURGER

54 LA LAMB BURGER

58 PP PULLED-PORK BURGER

60 HP HAM & PINEAPPLE BURGER

75 LO LOBSTER BURGER

76 PT PRAWN TOGARASHI BURGER

78 CR SOFT-SHELL CRAB BURGER

80 CM CLAM PO' BOY

84 HD CLASSIC HOT DOG

85 BD MAPLE-GLAZED BACON DOG

102 MC BAKED MACARONI WITH THREE CHEESES

104 PC POTATO CRISPS

105–109 MS MILKSHAKES

114 BB SOFT BURGER BUNS

115 BQ BARBECUE SAUCE

116 TK TOMATO KETCHUP

130 KS TOMATO KASUNDI

131 TQ TOMATO & QUINCE RELISH

132 BS BACON SALT

133 BT BEETROOT

136 PK PICKLES

137 CS CUCUMBER & SHALLOT PICKLE

36
WA
WAGYU
CHEESEBURGER
DELUXE

— PAGE NUMBER
— RECIPE SYMBOL
— RECIPE NAME

14
BP
BURGER PATTY

18
BC
BACON

36
WA
WAGYU
CHEESEBURGER
DELUXE

38
HS
HALF-SIZED
BURGER

40
WO
WORKS
BURGER

42
BE
BACON & EGG
BURGER

46
DC
DOUBLE
CHEESEBURGER
WITH BACON

47
SP
HOT & SPICY
DELUXE

62
TN
TONKATSU
PORK BURGER

64
TU
TURKEY
BURGER

66
HS
HONEY SOY
CHICKEN
BURGER

68
KA
KARAAGE
CHICKEN
BURGER

70
SN
CRUMBED
SNAPPER
BURGER

74
CK
CHICKPEA
BURGER

86
PS
PEPPERED
STEAK
BURGER

88
RE
THE REUBEN
BURGER

90
DO
DOUCHE
BURGER

92
WB
'WHICH BEER'
PROJECT

98
HC
HAND-CUT
CHIPS

100
ON
ONION RINGS

116
CK
CHERRY
KETCHUP

117
SM
SPICY
MUSTARD

117
CB
CLARIFIED
BUTTER

120–126
MN
MAYONNAISE
& VARIATIONS

127
OM
ONION
& MUSTARD
JAM

127
CO
CARAMELISED
ONION

139
TY
THANKS

140
IX
INDEX

WELCOME TO BURGER LAB

Burgers, who doesn't love them? Not many people, in my mind! The idea of meat in a bun with fixings and condiments is nothing new, but the quality and type of ingredients can greatly affect the outcome.

The most important thing to remember when making a burger is that it should be the sum of its parts, with each ingredient being much like an instrument in an orchestra. Allow each component to sing!

I grew up eating burgers and I like to think that the classic wagyu cheeseburger deluxe I serve in my restaurants is the love child of all of the burgers I loved growing up (and still love now)!

In the coming chapters you will see the classic burgers on the menu at my burger restaurants, plus lots of different ideas for delicious burgers featuring different cuisines and less traditional ingredients, such as soft-shell crab and sesame chicken. Some purists would argue that a burger must contain a beef patty and that all of the rest are actually sandwiches. You can make up your own mind on that one.

A little bit of history…

I was fortunate to do my formal chef training at Grand Rapids Community College in Grand Rapids, Michigan. As I'm sure you are aware, the grand old USA is the romantic birthplace of burgers, and you can get one on almost every street corner. From McDonalds to Burger King, to the classic diner burger and even the Daniel Boulud burger with braised short rib and foie gras in the patty, there are thousands of representations!

About a year after opening a restaurant with Dante Ruaine and Jeff Wong, Dante and I were having a late-night post-service drink at the restaurant (in Collingwood, a suburb of Melbourne, Australia). We decided that there were no decent burgers in the area, so why not open a burger shop that only had a small menu, but did things with a restaurant mindset, and at reasonable prices. The whole shtick was centered around quality and fresh ingredients.

We started with five burgers, which were beef only – no chicken, no fish, no vegetarian. We decided that having a liquor licence was the way to go, as lots of people like to have a beer with their burger.

Upon securing a site almost directly across the road from our first restaurant, we embarked on a lot of burger trials for staff meals at the restaurant. We heard no complaints, and forged ahead with building our first burger restaurant.

It opened in December 2011 and took off with unprecedented popularity. Since then, we have opened four more burger restaurants. We have also expanded the menu, adding a tofu burger and a fried chicken burger.

The goal of the restaurants and this book is to have fun. We have upbeat music in our restaurants, and young energetic staff who share our vision of quality and consistency. I hope you enjoy the recipes in this book, and are able to share the delicious results with your family and friends.

Daniel Wilson

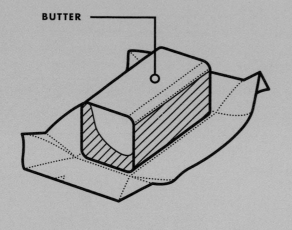

BUTTER

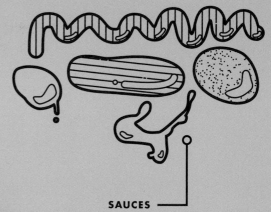

SAUCES

THE ELEMENTS

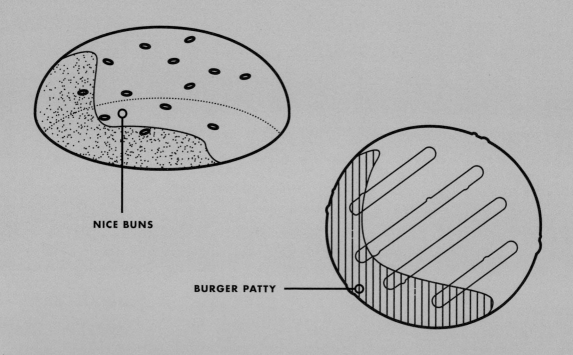

NICE BUNS

BURGER PATTY

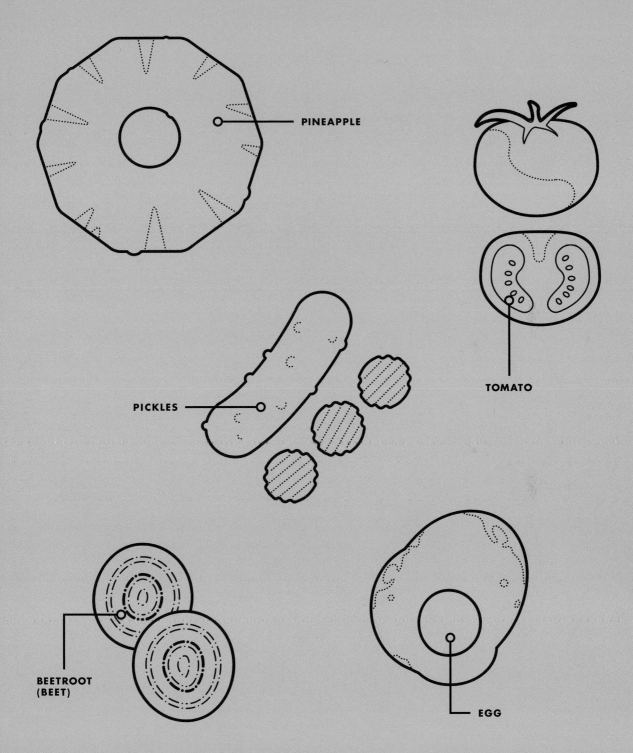

PINEAPPLE

TOMATO

PICKLES

BEETROOT
(BEET)

EGG

BUNS BU

The burger bun is one of the most important parts of the burger *(see Fig. 1)*. Its main purpose is to hold everything together and essentially provide the structure for the delicious ingredients inside.

The bun should be able to envelop all the fillings and be easy to bite through, without sending the ingredients flying out of the sides! A bun that is too thick or too hard will greatly diminish your burger-eating experience.

I am a firm believer in brushing the inside of the bun with clarified butter or olive oil and then toasting the cut surfaces on a flat grill to create a crisp golden crust on the inside; this also steams the bread, to help it compress around the ingredients.

Toasting the buns dry under a grill (broiler) can be counter-productive, as it can dry the bun out and make it too crispy and hard.

Here is a list of some classic bun types and their particular properties.

SESAME SEED BUN

The all-time classic. This bun is usually made from a white-flour dough and is round and low. It is commonly a little on the sweet side, to counterbalance salty charred meats.

BRIOCHE BUN

A yeast dough enriched with butter, brioche has become very popular recently. Some puritans feel that these are too sweet and rich for a burger, and can even tend towards being a little cake-like.

WHOLEMEAL/WHOLEGRAIN BUN

For the health conscious out there. A wholemeal (whole-wheat) or wholegrain bun can provide extra dietary fibre, but be careful as these can be more firm and dense than regular buns, and therefore may not provide the best burger experience.

PIDE (TURKISH BREAD)

Not a burger bun, so let's not even go there. Same with focaccia bread!

BUTTER ^{BT}

In my eyes, butter *(see Fig. 2)* is one of the most important ingredients in a burger. The key to making the bun extra delicious is to brush the inside of the bun with clarified butter (which is easy to make at home; see page 117) and then toast the bun on a flat grill. This has two benefits, other than the luscious addition of the butter itself.

1. Grilling the inside of the bun adds a toasty crispiness, which works brilliantly with the meat (or other filling) in the burger.

2. The other benefit is that grilling the buns steams them from the inside. This means that when the burger is assembled, the bun squashes around the filling like a perfect casing. This keeps all the ingredients inside nicely and ensures the focus is on the ingredients within, and stops the burger being too 'bready'!

There's nothing worse than eating a burger that is more like a rissole stuffed inside a loaf of bread. The burger should be a good representation of all its parts, without focusing too much on any single bit.

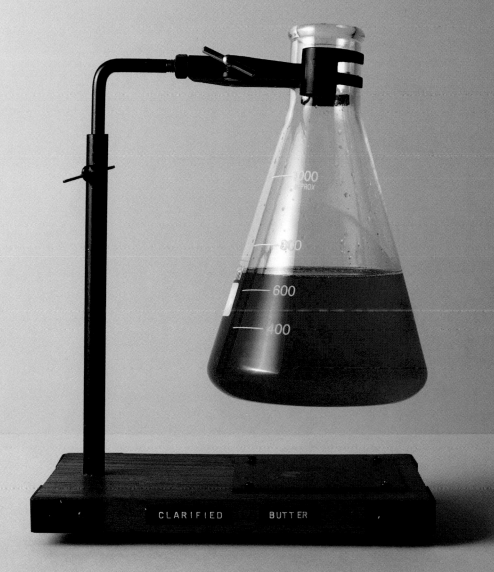

CLARIFIED   BUTTER

— Fig. 2 —

BURGER PATTY ^{BP}

The beef patty is the star of the burger *(see Fig 3)*. If the patty isn't good, then the whole burger is ruined!

When cooked, the patty must be the same diameter as the bun, as there's nothing worse than a patty that only fills up half the bun. Meat has a natural tendency to shrink when it's cooked, so it's important to take this into consideration when shaping the patties. I'd suggest that you shape the patties to be at least 20 per cent bigger than your buns.

In pursuit of the ultimate beef patty, let's now consider the merits of the different types and cuts of beef.

GRASS-FED VERSUS GRAIN-FED BEEF

When using regular beef, I prefer to use grass-fed as opposed to grain-fed – the main reason being that I think grass-fed is better for the cattle and the environment, as the cattle are free to roam and are not kept in feedlots. The meat also has the taste of where it comes from (terroir) and what the animal's diet is, which can often be identified as having a mineral flavour. Many farmers may also top up the feed with hay and silage harvested from the property after an abundance of spring growth.

Beef from grain-fed cattle can all taste the same, as the animals are essentially eating the same type of feed. The upside to grain-fed is the consistency of the marbling and tenderness of the meat; grass-fed beef can be a lot more variable in tenderness and marbling, due to the fact that the cattle roam more.

WAGYU BEEF

Wagyu literally means 'Japanese cow'. The special thing about these cattle is that they have a high amount of naturally occurring intramuscular marbling. This means that the fat is evenly dispersed inside the muscles, not just between them, creating deliciously juicy beef.

Wagyu beef can either be full-blood (pure-bred) or F1, which is a cross of full-blood and another breed, commonly Angus or Holstein, which bring their qualities to the beef. F1 is cheaper than full-blood.

The fat in wagyu beef is high in unsaturated fats, which means it is better for us, and also melts at a lower temperature. A good test for wagyu beef is to put a little of the fat on your thumbnail; it should melt from your body temperature.

Although the majority of wagyu beef is grain-fed, we use grass-fed wagyu for our patties, as it has an excellent flavour and retains moisture during cooking.

COMPOSITION OF THE PATTY

There are many schools of thought on the make-up of the patty. Some people swear it must have certain percentages of different cuts to make the perfect burger.

If you have a good relationship with your butcher, maybe you can ask them for specific muscles, although this may be tricky if you only want a small amount. If you have a mincer at home, you can get the cuts you want and grind the beef yourself.

When grinding your own meat, it is very important to keep the mincing equipment and the meat itself as cold as possible. If it warms up, the fat can start to melt, which will cause the meat to become dry, and crumble when cooked.

You really don't want more than about 20 per cent fat in the meat, otherwise you'll find that most of it just comes out during cooking. If you are cooking on a flat grill or pan, the meat will become crispy on the outside, yet greasy at the same time. If you use a flame-fired chargrill to cook the patties, it will flare up too much and give the patties an unappealing burnt-fat flavour. Personally I think 10–15 per cent fat is the sweet spot.

In our patties, we mainly use the muscles from the butt area – generally the silverside, topside and knuckle. These give a patty with good texture and mouth-feel, without too much sinew.

As you will see from the recipes, we add only salt and pepper to our patties. It comes down to personal preference, but some people like to add fillers such as onion, tomato sauce (ketchup), mustard, breadcrumbs, egg, etc – but I believe this detracts from the flavour of the beef itself, and can give the patties a pasty texture. Also, tomato sauce can make the patties burn excessively during cooking.

It is best to make and cook the patties on the day you plan to serve them. I would not recommend making a few and freezing them, as the juices will come out of them and they won't be great. Fresh is always best!

— Fig. 3 —

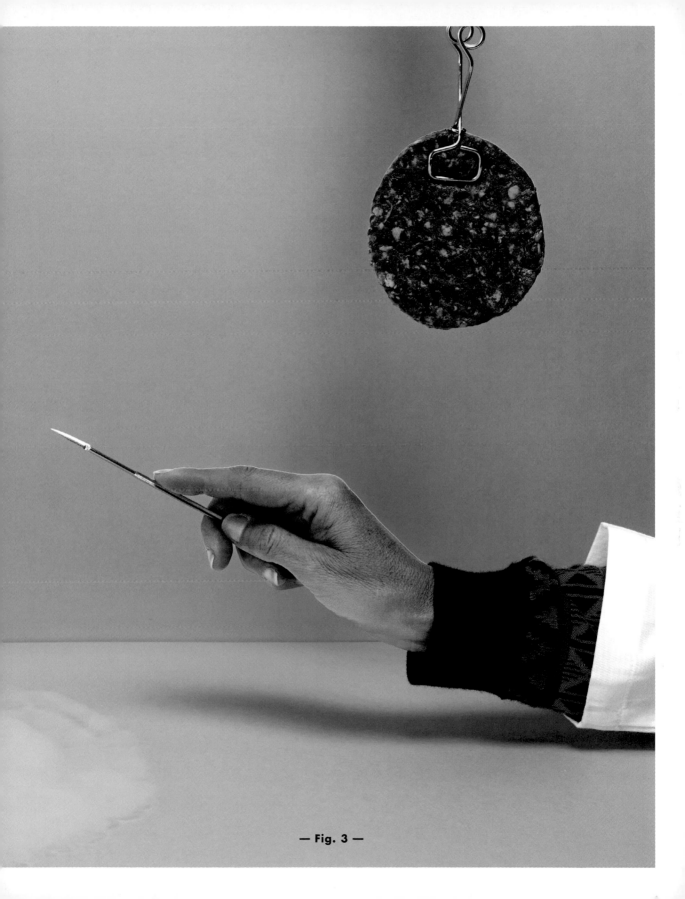

— Fig. 3 —

BACON ^{BC}

Bacon is one of the most adored additions to a burger *(see Fig. 4)*. There are a few types of bacon, and none of them are bad. While the typical American-style burger favours streaky bacon, you are more likely to see middle bacon in an Antipodean burger.

Bacon is simply cured meat from a pig – most often coming from the belly, but it can also come from the shoulder, loin, or loin and belly together. The meat is either brined or packed in salt to cure it, then smoked, with or without heat. It is then normally baked, grilled or fried before it finds its way into a burger.

Cheaper bacon can often be pumped full of water, which leaks out during cooking and can tend to make it soggy. As with all ingredients, for an utterly delicious result, I would suggest purchasing the best that you can find and afford.

Bacon is currently a very popular ingredient, and has made its way into a lot of sweet dishes recently – bacon jam, chocolate-covered bacon, bacon ice cream, and our own bacon maple milkshake syrup (see page 107).

Now for a quick look at the different tasty types of bacon.

KAISERFLEISCH (STREAKY BACON)

This is bacon from the belly. It is called streaky bacon because of the lines of meat and fat along it. Most of the fat renders during cooking and the meat becomes crispy. In the United States bacon is generally cooked until it is very crisp; personally, I like it a little softer.

KASSLER (CANADIAN) BACON

This bacon is cured and then hot-smoked, and usually made from the loin or neck. The advantage of this cut is that it is quite lean, but because of this it can dry out a little.

MIDDLE BACON

This consists of both the loin and the belly. Some might say it is the best of both worlds.

KASSLER
(CANADIAN)
BACON

MIDDLE
BACON

— Fig. 4 —

KETCHUP & MUSTARD ^{KM}

'BROTHERS IN ARMS'

Ketchup and mustard *(see Fig. 5)* are as important to a burger as the meat or the bun, in terms of the punchy flavours they add.

I think of the burgers in this book as old-school American-style burgers. We use Heinz ketchup and French's American mustard, as these are classic flavours associated with this type of burger. I guess this is in line with the old grammatically incorrect adage, 'If it ain't broke, don't fix it!' It's a reference point, and also has a comfort factor: when people recognise a certain flavour or food, it generally makes them happy and they feel good eating it.

Ketchup originally came from China and was a mix of pickled fish and spices called *ke-chiap*. The condiment we know today as ketchup (or 'catsup', as it is also called) was popularised in the United States in the nineteenth century, when it started being produced on a more commercial scale; the industry-standard Heinz variety has become famous the world over.

Mustard comes in many forms; see right for a quick rundown.

It's actually pretty simple to make your own ketchup and mustard – see the recipes on pages 116–117.

AMERICAN MUSTARD

Sometimes known as yellow mustard, this is the staple mustard for a classic burger. Commonly it is bright yellow due to the addition of turmeric, and a little sweet. It's good for kids, as it isn't too spicy.

HOT ENGLISH MUSTARD

This is similar in appearance to American mustard, but as the name states, this one is hot! It is made from darker and stronger mustard seeds than other mustards.

DIJON MUSTARD

Originally from Dijon in France, this mustard is made with white wine and is traditionally quite spicy. It has a light brown colour and is not protected by 'designation of origin' labelling laws, so these days it is made all over the world. It stands up well to more richly flavoured meats, also goes really well with chicken, and can be added to mayonnaise to make a dressing called 'dijonnaise'. If you like it extra spicy, look for 'dijon forte' (strong).

WHOLEGRAIN (OR 'SEED') MUSTARD

This mustard is typically quite mild, and the individual mustard seeds are left whole. It can be flavoured with different herbs and liquids.

HONEY MUSTARD

This sweet mustard goes well with chicken, and can be quite nice as a dressing for lettuce. A little bit goes a long way.

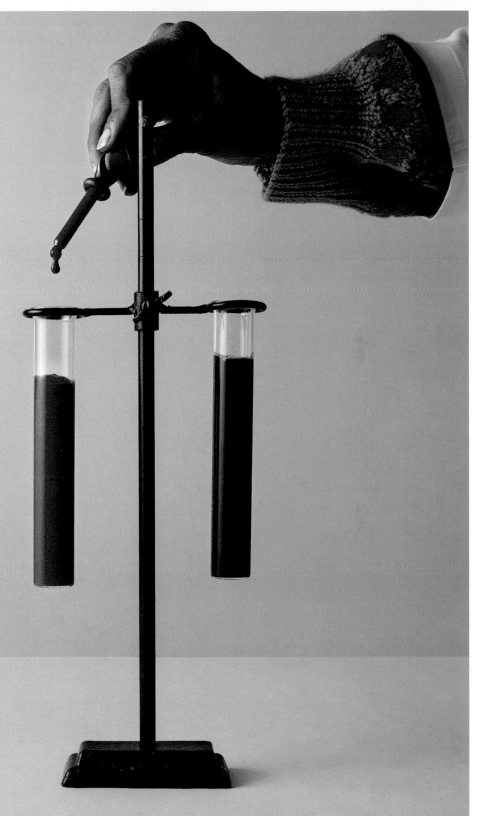

— Fig. 5 —

CHEESE ^{CH}

The cheeseburger is probably the most popular burger in the world. A good cheeseburger should have the cheese added to the top of the patty while it is still on the grill so it can melt and cover the top of the meat. There are several types of cheese commonly used for burgers *(see Fig. 6)*. You can pretty much use whatever you want! Here are some suggestions.

AMERICAN (PROCESSED) CHEESE

This orange cheese is probably the most commonly used on burgers. Processed cheese can be made from a single cheese (either solid, or freeze-dried and then powdered), or several cheeses. Cream, milk fat, water, salt, artificial colour, oils (for consistency and texture) and spices may also be added. The resulting mixture is heated with an emulsifier (to stop the oil and water separating), then poured into a mould and allowed to cool. It's a popular cheese as it's inexpensive, melts well and doesn't congeal.

If you are a lover of fine food only, then this particular cheese is probably a no-go zone!

SWISS CHEESE

This is the common name for the cooked-curd, medium-hard cheese that originated in Emmental, Switzerland. It has a distinct firm texture, sweet nutty flavour and characteristic holes, or 'eyes'. A great cheese to add a different flavour to your burgers, and a must for a Reuben (see page 88).

CHEDDAR

This hard, crumbly, sharp-tasting cheese originated in Cheddar, a village in the English county of Somerset. The process in which the curds are cut is known as 'cheddaring'. The cheese is commonly cloth-bound and aged, and over time the sweet, tangy, grassy flavours can develop into a sharp, acidic piquancy, with an earthy taste.

Proper cheddar does not melt very well and is quite expensive. Many other cheeses from all over the world are called cheddar and are more suited to burgers in terms of price and melting ability.

PEPPER JACK

This is a version of Monterey Jack, which is a semi-hard and slightly creamy cheese first made by Mexican Franciscan friars in Monterey, California. Pepper Jack is regular Monterey Jack, but with jalapeño or habanero chillies through it. It melts quite well and is perfect for chilli lovers!

MOZZARELLA

This southern Italian cheese is traditionally made from buffalo milk and is served fresh. The type more commonly used on pizzas and burgers is made from cow's milk and is pale yellow, rubbery and very stringy when heated. It is fairly inexpensive and mild in flavour.

BLUE CHEESE

Probably the most polarising cheese to regularly feature on a burger, but quite common in the United States. Generally when used it is a mild, creamy style that is crumbled on top of the patty.

MOZZARELLA

PEPPER JACK

SWISS

BLUE

CHEDDAR

AMERICAN

— Fig. 6 —

— Fig. 7 —

— Fig. 7 —

CHIPS ^{CI}

Chips are to burgers what barbecue sauce is to ribs. Chips and burgers fit hand in hand and belong together.

Before we look at the different types of chips *(see Fig. 7)*, let's go back to first principles and consider the humble potato.

The key to making the perfect chip is using a dry and mealy potato, as this creates chips that are crisp on the outside, but light and fluffy in the middle. If you use a waxy or starchy potato, you will find that your chips will brown without becoming crisp – so you'll end up with dark, soggy chips!

Here's a round-up of some good chipping potatoes; you'll find recipes for making your own simple hand-cut chips on page 98, and potato crisps on page 104.

EXCELLENT CHIPPING POTATOES

Russet burbank
Commonly known in North America as the Idaho potato, the russet burbank is a large potato with smooth dark skin and very few eyes. Its flesh is white, dry and mealy, making it ideal for chips and baked potatoes.

Sebago
The sebago is a very common all-rounder which makes great chips. It is sold in most supermarkets and greengrocers.

Bintje
A waxy potato, the bintje is an old Dutch variety with a lovely creamy, yellow flesh. It makes a beautiful potato salad and is also ideal for frying. This potato has a long shelf life.

Kennebec
An all-rounder and old favourite, with white firm flesh and thin skin. It is very popular for chips.

Coliban
A floury white-fleshed potato that is good for mashing, baking and roasting and is used to make French fries.

French fries

Also known as shoestring fries, these thin fries are very easy to eat and go perfectly with just about anything. Called *pommes frites* by the French, they are literally thin strips of fried potato. While there is continuing debate as to which is better, fresh or frozen, these days the French-fry technology is almost certainly in favour of the frozen variety, for its superior consistency and storage ability.

Straight-cut chips

This is the stock-standard chip sold in fish and chip shops. More often than not these chips are frozen, but more frequently these days you can find what is known as a 'hand-cut chip'. Generally these chips are cooked in two stages. They are either cooked whole and then cut and fried to order, or they're cut and blanched at a low oil temperature until lightly cooked through, but with no colour, and then finished at a normal oil temperature to crisp them up.

Crinkle-cut chips

A personal favourite. I have fond memories of these growing up. The beauty of the crinkle-cut is that there is more surface area, and therefore more crispness. These chips are almost always cooked from frozen, as they are more easily cut to shape by commercial food companies using specialist equipment.

Wedges

Well, if you really must... but they're not a real chip, in my opinion!

PICKLES ^{PK}

Pickles *(see Fig. 8)* are an essential part of a burger, in my view, as they help to balance out the rich fattiness of the beef. Not only excellent sliced inside a burger, they are alo fantastic served whole on the side.

The word 'pickle' comes from the Dutch word *pekel*, which means 'brine'. Although pickles can be made from just about any vegetable or fruit, traditionally they are small cucumbers that are brined and/or fermented, effectively as a means of preserving fresh cucumbers to last throughout the year. Just about every cuisine has their own version, and they are especially popular in Eastern Europe.

Some common modern preparations of pickles are battered and deep-fried pickles, as well as the 'pickleback' – a shot of Irish whiskey followed by a shot of pickle brine.

While you can buy excellent pickles, it is easy enough to make your own, and they'll keep for several months. See the recipe on page 136.

DILL (KOSHER) PICKLES

This is the most common type of pickle associated with burgers. Sour and crunchy, they are a New York–Jewish style of pickle that usually has a generous amount of fresh dill and garlic added to the brine. These pickles have been made in Poland, Russia, Ukraine and Germany for hundreds of years.

GHERKINS

These are made from a specific type of cucumber, known as the burr gherkin or West Indian gherkin. They are slightly smaller than regular pickled cucumbers and often a little sweeter. The term 'gherkin' has become a common name for smaller pickles that may not necessarily be made from actual burr gherkins.

CORNICHONS

These are the tiny French gherkins, which are pickled in wine vinegar and tarragon. They are quite tart and commonly served with terrines and pâtés.

BRINED PICKLES

These are naturally fermented pickles without the addition of vinegar. The lactobacillus bacteria naturally found on the skin of the cucumber is responsible for kicking off the lacto-fermentation, which turns the cucumber sour. The cucumbers are placed in a 2–4% salt brine and left to ferment.

— Fig. 8 —

THE SALAD BITS ^{SL}

LETTUCE

Ah, the leafy greens. It's often said that you don't win friends with salad; I don't necessarily agree with this. I love a good crisp leaf *(see Fig. 9)*, and like to use different ones for different purposes.

With food we are always looking for balance, and lettuce is often a foil to the richness of the meat in a burger. Some people even use it as a wrap for the burger fillings when gluten or carbs are being avoided.

Washing lettuce is very important as it can often be gritty or sandy. Even more important than washing it is drying it – the last thing you want to do is add wet lettuce to your carefully constructed burger. Salad spinners are inexpensive and easy to use.

Iceberg lettuce
Iceberg lettuce is the old faithful of the lettuce world, often looked down upon in these times of gourmet salad mixes and micro greens. I find iceberg lettuce hard to beat for its refreshing flavour and texture, and its quality is very good year round too. Always discard the outer leaves and get rid of the tough white ribs – the light green pieces are the best.

Cos (romaine) lettuce
Best known for being the main ingredient in a caesar salad, cos lettuce has a wonderful crunch to it, and the ribs are actually quite nice to eat. I'd recommend thinly slicing it before adding it to a burger, as the long pointy leaves are not really the right shape to sit inside a bun.

Butter (bibb) lettuce
Butter lettuce has a lovely soft leaf with little texture, but quite a lovely, delicate flavour. I think it is more suited to subtle flavours such as seafood. It is also quite fragile, so be very gentle when working with it as it bruises easily.

ROCKET (ARUGULA)

Rocket was the lettuce of the '90s. This small dark green leaf has a lovely peppery bite. It goes especially well with strongly flavoured foods such as lamb or game. The long, wiry stalk is best picked off before using.

KALE

This dark green curly leaf is so insanely popular with the hipster and vegetarian communities that it demands inclusion. It can be eaten raw, lightly blanched in boiling salted water, or even fried or dried. It is packed full of healthy vitamins and antioxidants.

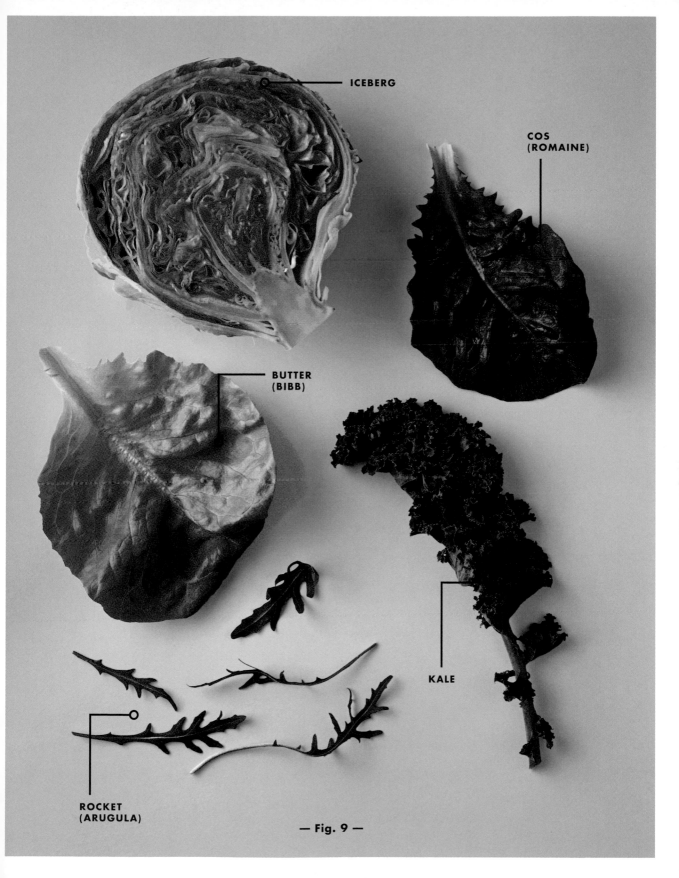

ICEBERG

COS
(ROMAINE)

BUTTER
(BIBB)

KALE

ROCKET
(ARUGULA)

— Fig. 9 —

THE OTHER BITS ^{OT}

Once we've taken care of the bun, meat, pickles, cheese, salad leaves and sauces, then come 'the other bits' *(see Fig 10)*. Tastes and preferences can vary greatly when it comes to these burger additions, so here's a guide to help you choose which ones *you* most like.

PINEAPPLE

Ah, the old Hawaiian burger. Growing up, I was quite fond of this delight, sold at the local fish and chip shop. Back in those days, tinned rings of pineapple were *de rigueur*, but I prefer to use fresh pineapple that is cut daily.

Much like tomato, hot pineapple can be a turn-off for some. We cook our pineapple on the flat grill, which gives it a nice charred flavour, but if you prefer you can just add it fresh.

TOMATO

Tomato is one of those funny ingredients that can be a real polariser. Some like it hot, some like it cold, and others just plain don't want it in there! We use regular vine-ripened tomatoes and slice them fresh every day.

BEETROOT (BEET)

The natural sweetness of the beetroot and piquancy of the vinegar it is pickled in is the perfect foil for the fattiness of the meat.

At the restaurant, we make our own beetroot several times a week and offer it as an extra on all burgers. I certainly do have a soft spot for it myself! See page 133 for our recipe.

EGG

Another Antipodean favourite... I love the feeling of egg yolk running between my fingers, spilling out the side of a burger. When having an egg in a burger, the egg must be fried, and the yolk must be runny. Some like to serve an open burger so the egg can be on show; either way it's all good to me.

Always buy free-range eggs and the best ones you can afford. Cook them in a non-stick frying pan with a little butter or olive oil, and make sure the pan is not too hot, as you don't want the edges of the egg white to be crispy.

PINEAPPLE

BEETROOT (BEET)

TOMATO

EGG

— Fig. 10 —

CLASSIC COMBOS

CROWD-PLEASERS

CLASSIC BURGERS

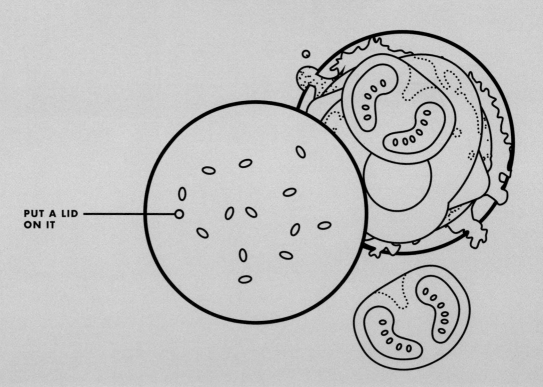

PUT A LID ON IT

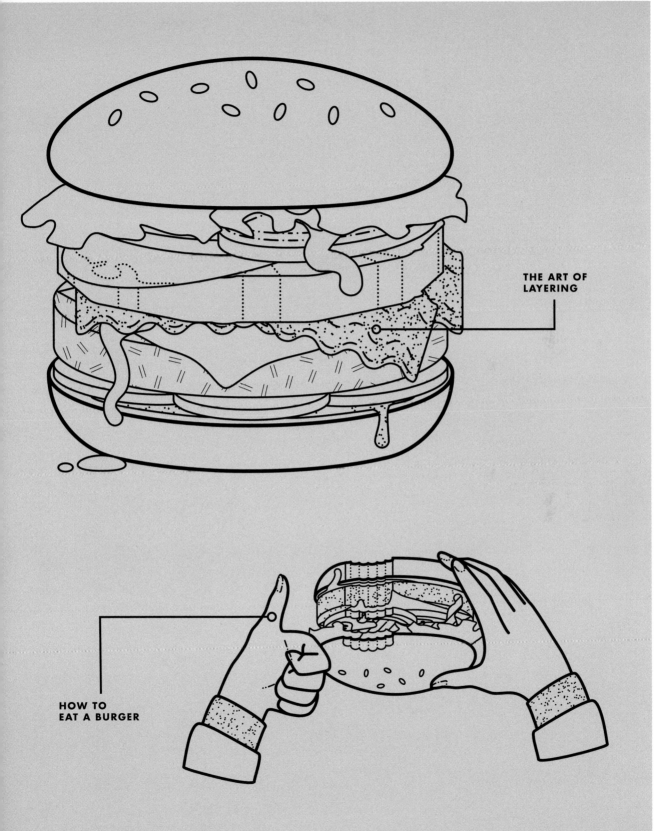

THE ART OF
LAYERING

HOW TO
EAT A BURGER

WAGYU CHEESEBURGER DELUXE ^{WA}

Here is our standard burger, from which all the others derive *(see Fig. 11)*. Remember to make sure the pan is hot enough to caremalise the meat nicely. You might like to serve the lettuce and tomato on the side, for people to add as they wish. Just make sure you don't skimp on the condiments!

MAKES 4

1 heaped teaspoon sea salt
¼ teaspoon freshly ground
    black pepper
400 g (14 oz) minced
    (ground) wagyu beef
4 slices cheddar
4 soft burger buns (see
    page 10), cut in half
melted clarified butter
    (page 117), for brushing

tomato ketchup (page 116)
20 pickle slices (page 136)
spicy mustard (page 117)
4 large tomato slices
4 iceberg lettuce leaves,
    washed, dried and torn
basic mayo (page 120)

BUILD FROM THE BOTTOM, IN THIS ORDER:

Bun bottom → Ketchup → Pickles → Cheese-topped patty →
Mustard → Tomato → Lettuce → Bun top, spread with mayo

INSTRUCTIONS

1   Mix the salt and pepper through the beef. Weigh out the mixture into four 100 g (3½ oz) portions and flatten them to about 1 cm (½ in) thick. Lay the patties on a sheet of baking paper.

2   Heat a flat grill plate, or a large non-stick frying pan, to a medium heat. Cook the patties for about 4 minutes on the first side, then turn them over and place a slice of cheese on each patty. Cook for a further 4 minutes, or until cooked through.

3   Brush the insides of the buns with clarified butter and toast lightly on the grill, then build your burgers.

— Fig. 11 —

HALF-SIZED BURGER ^{HS}

This one is for the kids. Essentially it is a mini wagyu cheeseburger deluxe, but without the pickles and mustard *(see Fig. 12)*.

MAKES 4

½ teaspoon sea salt
large pinch of freshly ground
    black pepper
200 g (7 oz) minced (ground)
    wagyu beef
2 slices cheddar, cut in half
4 soft burger buns (see
    page 10), cut in half

melted clarified butter
    (page 117), for brushing
tomato ketchup (page 116)
4 small tomato slices
2 iceberg lettuce leaves,
    washed, dried and torn
basic mayo (page 120)

BUILD FROM THE BOTTOM, IN THIS ORDER:

Bun bottom → Ketchup → Cheese-topped patty → Tomato →
Lettuce → Bun top, spread with mayo

INSTRUCTIONS

1 Mix the salt and pepper through the beef. Weigh out the mixture into four 50 g (1¾ oz) portions and flatten them to about 1 cm (½ in) thick. Lay the patties on a sheet of baking paper.

2 Heat a flat grill plate, or a non-stick frying pan, to a medium heat. Cook the patties for about 4 minutes on the first side, then turn them over and place a slice of cheese on each patty. Cook for a further 4 minutes, or until cooked through.

3 Brush the insides of the buns with clarified butter and toast lightly on the grill, then build your burgers.

— Fig. 12 —

WORKS BURGER ^{WO}

This is the one with the lot *(see Fig. 13)*. It's not the tidiest burger to eat as the sauces, juices and runny yolk come from all directions! However, it is bloody delicious.

MAKES 4

1 heaped teaspoon sea salt
¼ teaspoon freshly ground
   black pepper
400 g (14 oz) minced
   (ground) wagyu beef
4 slices cheddar
4 free-range eggs
8 slices kaiserfleisch
   (streaky bacon)
4 slices pineapple
4 soft burger buns (see
   page 10), cut in half

melted clarified butter
   (page 117), for brushing
tomato ketchup (page 116)
20 pickle slices (page 136)
spicy mustard (page 117)
4 large beetroot slices
   (page 133)
4 large tomato slices
4 iceberg lettuce leaves,
   washed, dried and torn
basic mayo (page 120)

BUILD FROM THE BOTTOM, IN THIS ORDER:

Bun bottom → Ketchup → Pickles → Cheese-topped patty →
Mustard → Bacon → Pineapple → Tomato → Egg → Beetroot →
Lettuce → Bun top, spread with mayo

INSTRUCTIONS

1 Heat the oven to a low setting.

2 Mix the salt and pepper through the beef. Weigh out the mixture into four 100 g (3½ oz) portions and flatten them to about 1 cm (½ in) thick. Lay the patties on a sheet of baking paper.

3 Heat a flat grill plate, or a large non-stick frying pan, to a medium heat. Cook the patties for about 4 minutes on the first side, then turn them over and place a slice of cheese on each patty. Cook for a further 4 minutes, or until cooked through. Place the patties on a baking tray and keep them warm in the oven.

4 Now cook the eggs, bacon and pineapple on the grill, or in the pan, transferring them to the oven to keep warm. (An extra non-stick frying pan would come in handy here, if you have one.) Simply fry the bacon for a few minutes on each side, until just crisp. The eggs should be cooked just until the sunny-side-up stage – about 2–3 minutes. The pineapple slices will only need a minute or so on each side.

5 Brush the insides of the buns with clarified butter and toast lightly on the grill, then build your burgers.

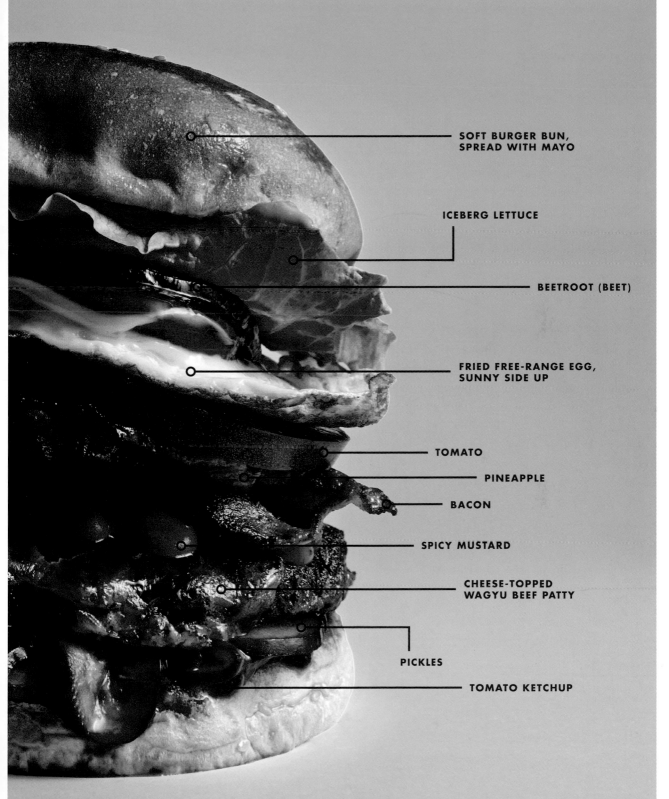

SOFT BURGER BUN,
SPREAD WITH MAYO

ICEBERG LETTUCE

BEETROOT (BEET)

FRIED FREE-RANGE EGG,
SUNNY SIDE UP

TOMATO

PINEAPPLE

BACON

SPICY MUSTARD

CHEESE-TOPPED
WAGYU BEEF PATTY

PICKLES

TOMATO KETCHUP

— Fig. 13 —

BACON & EGG BURGER ^{BE}

This burger came along with the opening of our city store. Given the number of corporate types rushing to work every morning past this store, we decided we needed a breakfast burger *(see Fig. 14)*. You can use either ketchup or barbecue sauce on this one; we prefer barbecue sauce.

MAKES 4

8 slices kaiserfleisch
   (streaky bacon)
4 free-range eggs
4 slices cheddar
4 soft burger buns (see
   page 10), cut in half
melted clarified butter
   (page 117), for brushing

tomato ketchup (page 116)
   or barbecue sauce
   (page 115)
125 g (4½ oz/½ cup) bloody
   mary mayo (page 125)

BUILD FROM THE BOTTOM, IN THIS ORDER:

Bun bottom → Ketchup or barbecue sauce → Bacon →
Egg with cheese → Bun top, spread with bloody mary mayo

INSTRUCTIONS

1 Heat the oven to a low setting.

2 Heat a flat grill plate, or a large non-stick frying pan, to a medium heat. Cook the bacon for 2–3 minutes on each side, until just crisp. Transfer to the oven to keep warm.

3 Cook the eggs for about 2 minutes on the first side, then flip them over and put a slice of cheese on each. Cook for another 1 minute, then keep warm in the oven.

4 Brush the insides of the buns with clarified butter and toast lightly on the grill, then build your burgers.

— Fig. 14 —

DOUBLE CHEESEBURGER
WITH BACON DC

SOFT BURGER BUN

ICEBERG LETTUCE

BASIC MAYO

TOMATO

SPICY MUSTARD

CHEESE-TOPPED WAGYU
BEEF PATTY No.2

CRISPY BACON

CHEESE-TOPPED WAGYU
BEEF PATTY No.1

PICKLES

BARBECUE SAUCE

RECIPE PAGE 46

— Fig. 15 —

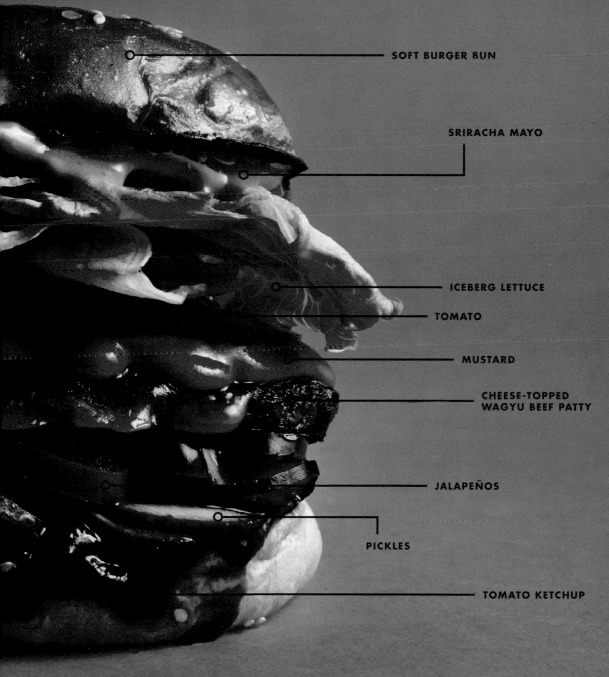

HOT & SPICY DELUXE ^{SP}

SOFT BURGER BUN

SRIRACHA MAYO

ICEBERG LETTUCE

TOMATO

MUSTARD

CHEESE-TOPPED
WAGYU BEEF PATTY

JALAPEÑOS

PICKLES

TOMATO KETCHUP

RECIPE PAGE 47

— Fig. 16 —

DOUBLE CHEESEBURGER WITH BACON ^{DC}

A big meaty, cheesy burger with barbecue sauce *(see Fig 15)*. This is definitely not one for the faint-hearted!

MAKES 4

2 teaspoons sea salt
½ teaspoon freshly ground
    black pepper
800 g (1 lb 12 oz) minced
    (ground) wagyu beef
8 slices cheddar
8 slices kaiserfleisch
    (streaky bacon)
4 soft burger buns (see
    page 10), cut in half

melted clarified butter
    (page 117), for brushing
barbecue sauce (page 115)
20 pickle slices (page 136)
spicy mustard (page 117)
4 large tomato slices
4 iceberg lettuce leaves,
    washed, dried and torn
basic mayo (page 120)

BUILD FROM THE BOTTOM, IN THIS ORDER:

Bun bottom → Barbecue sauce → Pickles → Patty #1 with cheese →
Bacon → Patty #2 with cheese → Mustard → Tomato → Lettuce →
Bun top, spread with mayo

INSTRUCTIONS

1 Heat the oven to a low setting.

2 Mix the salt and pepper through the beef. Weigh out the mixture into eight 100 g (3½ oz) portions and flatten them to about 1 cm (½ in) thick. Lay the patties on a sheet of baking paper.

3 Heat a flat grill plate, or a large non-stick frying pan, to a medium heat. Cook the patties (in batches if you need to) for about 4 minutes on the first side, then turn them over and place a slice of cheese on each patty. Cook for a further 4 minutes, or until cooked through. Place the patties on a baking tray and keep them warm in the oven.

4 Now cook the bacon for a few minutes on each side, until just crisp. Transfer to the oven to keep warm.

5 Brush the insides of the buns with clarified butter and toast lightly on the grill, then build your burgers.

HOT AND SPICY DELUXE ^{SP}

This is a hot one, and our second-most popular burger *(see Fig. 16)*.

MAKES 4

1 heaped teaspoon sea salt
¼ teaspoon freshly ground
    black pepper
400 g (14 oz) minced (ground)
    wagyu beef
4 slices cheddar
4 soft burger buns (see
    page 10), cut in half
melted clarified butter
    (page 117), for brushing

tomato ketchup (page 116)
20 pickle slices (page 136)
jalapeño chillies
spicy mustard (page 117)
4 large tomato slices
4 iceberg lettuce leaves,
    washed, dried and torn
sriracha mayo (page 121)

BUILD FROM THE BOTTOM, IN THIS ORDER:

Bun bottom → Ketchup → Pickles → Jalapeños →
Cheese-topped patty → Mustard → Tomato → Lettuce →
Bun top, spread with sriracha mayo

INSTRUCTIONS

1 Mix the salt and pepper through the beef. Weigh out the mixture into four 100 g (3½ oz) portions and flatten them to about 1 cm (½ in) thick. Lay the patties on a sheet of baking paper.

2 Heat a flat grill plate, or a large non-stick frying pan, to a medium heat. Cook the patties for about 4 minutes on the first side, then turn them over and place a slice of cheese on each patty. Cook for a further 4 minutes, or until cooked through.

3 Brush the insides of the buns with clarified butter and toast lightly on the grill, then build your burgers.

FRIED CHICKEN BURGER ^{FC}

The key to the fried chicken burger
(see Fig. 17) is juicy chicken and lots of mayo.
The thigh is the best part of the chicken, as it
has more flavour and isn't dry like the breast.
The chicken needs to marinate overnight, but
try not to make the slaw too far ahead, as it
will leach liquid and go a little soggy.

MAKES 4

200 ml (7 fl oz) buttermilk,
or 200 ml (7 fl oz) milk
with 1 teaspoon lemon
juice added
4 boneless, skinless
chicken thighs
vegetable oil, for deep-frying
4 soft burger buns (see
page 10), cut in half
melted clarified butter
(page 117), for brushing

Slaw
¼ small cabbage, thinly sliced
1 carrot, grated
½ red onion, thinly sliced
½ bunch (50 g/1¾ oz) flat-leaf
(Italian) parsley, thinly sliced
1 tablespoon celery seeds
125 g (4½ oz/½ cup) basic
mayo (page 120)
1 tablespoon red wine vinegar
2 teaspoons sugar

Jalapeño mayo
150 g (5½ oz) Kewpie
(Japanese) mayonnaise
2 tablespoons jalapeño
chilli sauce, or to taste

Spiced flour
1 teaspoon cayenne pepper
1 teaspoon ground turmeric
3 teaspoons sweet paprika
2 teaspoons salt
3 teaspoons ground cumin
1 teaspoon Chinese five-spice
3 teaspoons cornflour
(cornstarch)
2 teaspoons garlic powder
2 teaspoons onion powder
3 teaspoons ground
sichuan pepper
2 teaspoons ground
white pepper
150 g (5½ oz/1 cup) plain
(all-purpose) flour

BUILD FROM THE BOTTOM, IN THIS ORDER:

Bun bottom → Slaw → Chicken → Bun top, spread
with jalapeño mayo

INSTRUCTIONS

1 Pour the buttermilk into a large bowl or dish
and add the chicken thighs. Cover and refrigerate
overnight. This will tenderise the chicken and
make it extra juicy.

2 For the jalapeño mayo, whisk the mayonnaise
and chilli sauce together and set aside. You can
add more or less of the chilli sauce depending
on how spicy you like it.

3 For the slaw, mix all the ingredients together. Season
well with salt and freshly ground black pepper.

4 For the spiced flour, mix all the ingredients together
in a large bowl.

5 To serve, heat about 10 cm (4 in) of oil in a large
saucepan, to about 175°C (345°F). You can test
by dipping a wooden chopstick in – the oil should
sizzle when ready.

6 Remove the chicken thighs from the buttermilk.
Toss well with the spiced flour, then shake off
the excess using a sieve.

7 Gently lower the chicken into the hot oil and fry
for 5–6 minutes, or until golden, crisp and cooked
through. Drain immediately on paper towel.

8 To assemble the burgers, heat a flat grill plate,
or a non-stick frying pan, to a medium heat. Brush
the insides of the buns with clarified butter and toast
lightly on the grill, then build your burgers.

SOFT BURGER BUN

JALAPEÑO MAYO

CRISP-FRIED SPICED
CHICKEN THIGH

SLAW

— Fig. 17 —

ORGANIC TOFU BURGER ^{TO}

After a year of serving burgers made only from beef, we decided to add a vegetarian offering *(see Fig. 18)*. We decided to use a sesame and yuzu mayo on this one, as the nuttiness of the sesame seeds works well with the tofu.

MAKES 4

1 tablespoon vegetable oil
4 slices organic firm tofu, each
    about 1 cm (½ in) thick
4 slices cheddar
4 soft burger buns (see
    page 10), cut in half
melted clarified butter
    (page 117), for brushing

60 g (2 oz/¼ cup) sesame
    & yuzu mayo (page 121)
4 large tomato slices
4 iceberg lettuce leaves,
    washed, dried and torn

BUILD FROM THE BOTTOM, IN THIS ORDER:

Bun bottom → Sesame & yuzu mayo → Cheese-topped tofu →
Tomato → Lettuce → Bun top, spread with sesame & yuzu mayo

INSTRUCTIONS

1 Heat the oil in a large non-stick frying pan over a medium heat. Cook the tofu for about 2–3 minutes on the first side, then turn the tofu over and place a slice of cheese on each. Cook for a further 2–3 minutes, or until heated through. Remove and keep warm.

2 Brush the insides of the buns with clarified butter and toast lightly in the pan, then build your burgers.

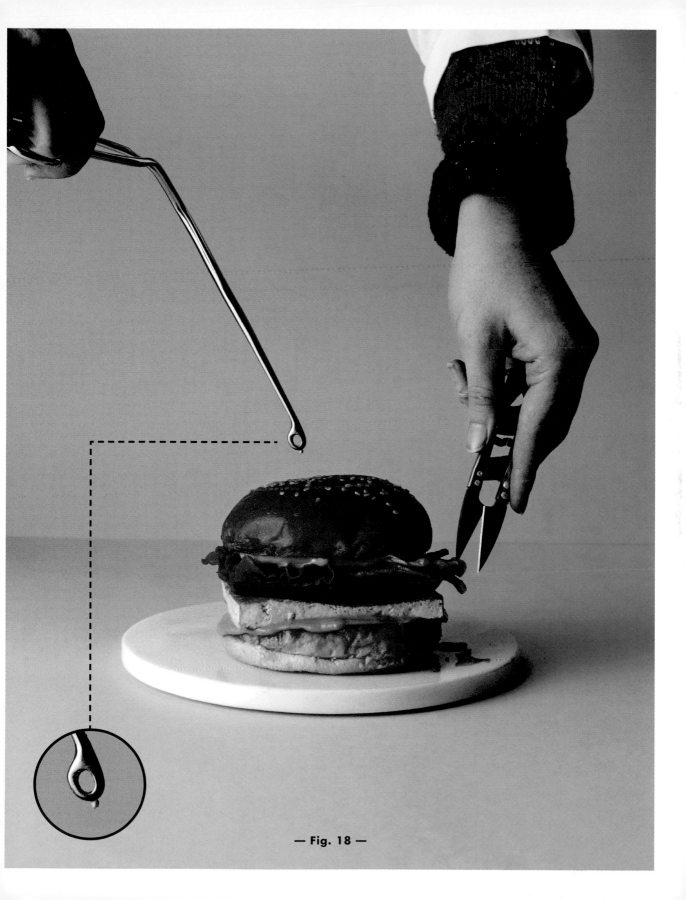

— Fig. 18 —

HOW TO EAT A BURGER ^{EB}

(1) Inspect the finished burger.

(2) Make sure 'all hands are inside the vehicle' (i.e. no ingredients are hanging out) prior to picking up.

(5) Take a big bite and enjoy.

(6) Put the burger down on its lid, and then pick up the same way to take another bite.

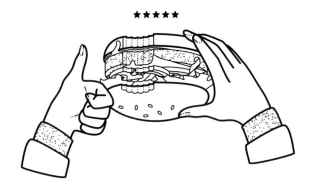

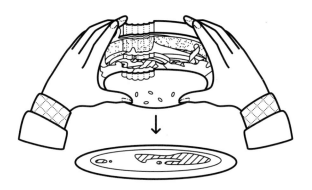

③ Press the top of the burger down, so it is all nicely compressed and ready to eat.

④ Pick the burger up, with your hands turned over, so it is upside down when you pick it up.

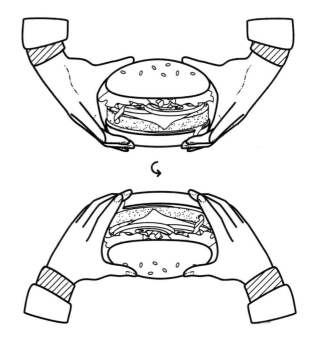

⑦ When you still have a couple of bites to go, use the burger to mop up all the juices and enjoy the final few bites.

⑧ Burger complete! Repeat steps as necessary.

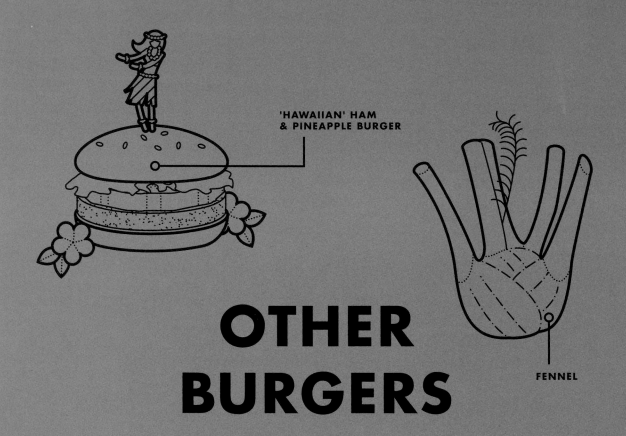

'HAWAIIAN' HAM
& PINEAPPLE BURGER

FENNEL

OTHER
BURGERS

LOBSTER

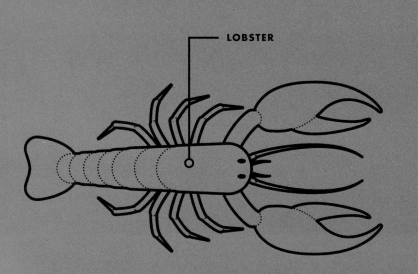

SWISS CHEESE

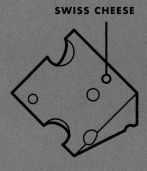

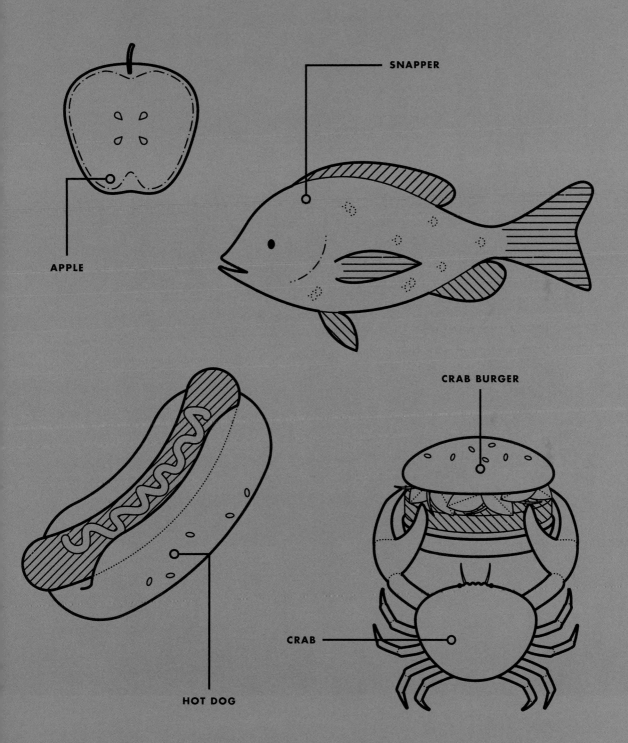

APPLE

SNAPPER

CRAB BURGER

HOT DOG

CRAB

LAMB BURGER WITH MINT YOGHURT AND PICKLED CUCUMBER ^{LA}

A Greek-style burger (see Fig. 19) packed full of flavour. You'll need to make the minted yoghurt and super-simple cucumber pickle a day ahead, but they're worth it for this delicious lamb burger.

MAKES 4 BURGERS

1½ teaspoons sea salt
½ teaspoon freshly ground
   black pepper
500 g (1 lb 2 oz) minced
   (ground) lamb, not too
   lean and not too fatty
olive oil, for drizzling
4 tablespoons tomato kasundi
   (page 130)
35 g (1¼ oz/1 cup) rocket
   (arugula) leaves
4 soft burger buns (see
   page 10), cut in half

Mint yoghurt
250 g (9 oz/1 cup)
   Greek-style yoghurt
2 tablespoons mint, chopped
1 garlic clove, minced

Pickled cucumber
1 Lebanese (short)
   cucumber
2 tablespoons white
   wine vinegar
2 tablespoons sugar

BUILD FROM THE BOTTOM, IN THIS ORDER:

Bun bottom → Tomato kasundi → Lamb patty → Rocket →
Pickled cucumber → Mint yoghurt → Bun top

INSTRUCTIONS

1 For the mint yoghurt, put the yoghurt in a fine-mesh sieve set over a bowl. Leave to drain in the fridge overnight. Next day, near serving time, mix the mint and garlic through the yoghurt and season to taste with sea salt and freshly ground black pepper. Set aside at room temperature.

2 For the pickled cucumber, peel the cucumber and remove the ends. Now use the peeler to peel strips the length of the cucumber on each side, until you reach the seeds. Once you have peeled all the flesh off, discard the seeds. Toss the cucumber strips with a good pinch of sea salt and leave for 15 minutes. Bring the vinegar, sugar and 2 tablespoons water to the boil. Once the sugar has dissolved, set aside to cool, then pour over the cucumber. Cover and leave in the fridge for at least 2 hours, or preferably overnight; the pickles will keep for up to 2 months in the fridge. Drain on paper towel before serving.

3 For the patties, mix the salt and pepper through the lamb. Weigh out the mixture into four 125 g (4½ oz) portions and flatten them to about 1 cm (½ in) thick. Lay the patties on a sheet of baking paper.

4 To serve, heat a cast-iron grill pan over a medium heat and lightly oil it. Cook the patties for 90 seconds, then turn them around 90 degrees on the same side, to give nice cross-hatch marks underneath. Leave them to cook for another 90 seconds. Now turn the patties over and repeat on the other side, leaving them for 90 seconds, before turning them 90 degrees and cooking for a final 90 seconds. Remove from the pan and keep somewhere warm.

5 Brush the insides of the buns with olive oil and toast lightly on the grill, then build your burgers.

SOFT BURGER BUN

MINT YOGHURT

PICKLED CUCUMBER

ROCKET (ARUGULA)

LAMB PATTY

TOMATO KASUNDI

— Fig. 19 —

SMOKED PULLED-PORK BURGER WITH PICKLES ^{PP}

This burger features a classic South Carolina–style barbecue pulled pork *(see Fig. 20)*. There's a bit of a process involved in smoking the pork, so even if you don't have seven buddies to help you eat all the burgers, it's worth cooking the entire quantity of pork and reserving some for another use, as the result is well worth the effort. You can use an old pot or wok to smoke the pork in, but do try to do the smoking outside as you don't want to stink your house out. Enjoy with a frosty beer.

MAKES 8

1 kg (2 lb 3 oz) boneless pork shoulder or neck
1 cup wood chips, preferably hickory or mesquite
250–500 ml (8½–17 fl oz/ 1–2 cups) barbecue sauce (page 115)

8 soft burger buns (see page 10), cut in half
melted clarified butter (page 117), for brushing
48 pickle slices (page 136)

BUILD FROM THE BOTTOM, IN THIS ORDER:

Bun bottom → Pickles → Pulled pork → Bun top

INSTRUCTIONS

1 Remove the pork from the fridge about 30 minutes before smoking, to bring it to room temperature.

2 Get an old pot or wok and line the bottom with foil. Sprinkle the wood chips onto the foil, then place a couple of racks in the bottom to create some distance between the wood chips and the pork.

3 Place the pot or wok on a small butane burner that uses gas cartridge bottles (cheap to buy from Asian grocery stores). Turn the burner on high, so that the chips start to flare and turn into smoking embers.

4 Place the pork on the racks and turn the heat down to low. Cover the pot or wok tightly with foil. Then turn the pork every 15 minutes for an hour. This is hot smoking, but we want to do it quite gently.

5 To braise the pork, preheat the oven to 150°C (300°F). Remove the pork from the smoker and place in a baking dish. Pour in 100 ml (3½ fl oz) water and cover with foil. Now braise in the oven for 2–3 hours, until the pork is fork-tender. Remove from the oven and let cool slightly. While it is still warm, put some disposable gloves on and gently break the pork apart with your fingers, removing and discarding any large fatty bits, and place in a bowl. Add enough barbecue sauce so the pork is nicely coated, but not swimming in sauce.

6 To assemble, gently reheat the pork over a low heat; you may need to add a little more barbecue sauce or water if the meat has absorbed the liquid and become a little dry.

7 Heat a flat grill plate, or large non-stick frying pan, to a medium heat. Brush the insides of the buns with clarified butter and toast lightly on the grill, then build your burgers.

— Fig. 20 —

GRILLED HAM & PINEAPPLE BURGER WITH CHIPOTLE MAYO ^{HP}

While most hamburgers have absolutely no ham anywhere near them, this is a real 'ham' burger. I guess it could be called a Hawaiian burger, as is usually the case whenever ham and pineapple are teamed up. The chipotle mayo adds a bit of spice and smokiness to complement the ham *(see Fig. 21)*.

MAKES 4

4 ham steaks, roughly
    the size of the burger
    buns if possible
vegetable oil, for brushing
4 slices fresh pineapple,
    core removed
4 soft burger buns (see
    page 10), cut in half

melted clarified butter
    (page 117), for brushing
125 g (4½ oz/½ cup) chipotle
    mayo (page 124)
4 iceberg lettuce leaves,
    washed, dried and finely
    shredded

BUILD FROM THE BOTTOM, IN THIS ORDER:

Bun bottom → Chipotle mayo → Lettuce → Pineapple →
Ham → Bun top

INSTRUCTIONS

1 Heat a cast-iron grill plate, or frying pan, to a medium–high heat. Brush the ham steaks with a little oil and then cook for about 2 minutes on each side. Set aside and keep warm, then cook the pineapple in the same way.

2 Meanwhile, heat a large non-stick frying pan, or flat grill plate, to a medium heat. Brush the insides of the buns with clarified butter and toast lightly on the grill, then build your burgers and dream of the sunny shores of Hawaii...

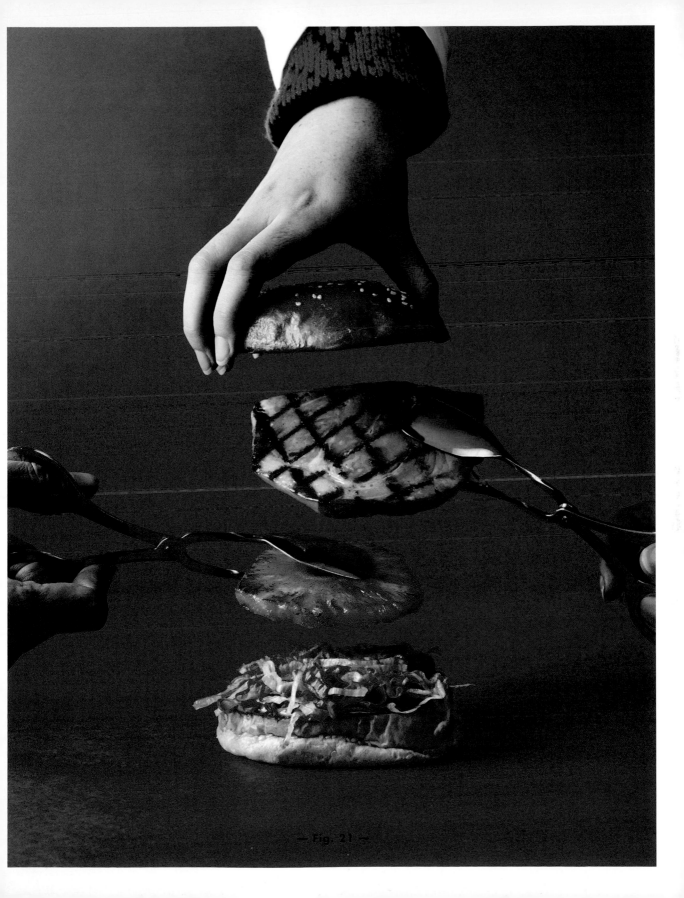

— Fig. 21 —

TONKATSU PORK BURGER WITH APPLE & FENNEL SLAW ᵀᴺ

Let's be honest: crumbing food makes just it better! Japanese crumbed pork (tonkatsu) is bloody delicious. Even better is tonkatsu sauce, which is basically Japanese barbecue sauce, widely available from Asian grocers, along with the panko breadcrumbs. Throw in some slaw and some buns and you've got a real crowd pleaser *(see Fig. 22)*.

MAKES 4

vegetable oil, for deep-frying
4 soft burger buns (see
    page 10), cut in half
150 g (5½ oz) tonkatsu mayo
    (page 123)

Fennel & apple slaw

1 fennel bulb, shaved
1 green apple, peeled
    and grated
¼ red cabbage, thinly sliced
125 g (4½ oz/½ cup) basic
    mayo (page 120)

Tonkatsu pork

500 g (1 lb 2 oz) pork loin,
    trimmed of all sinew
1 free-range egg
125 ml (4 fl oz/½ cup) milk
plain (all-purpose) flour,
    for dusting
120 g (4½ oz/2 cups) panko
    (Japanese) breadcrumbs

BUILD FROM THE BOTTOM, IN THIS ORDER:

Bun bottom → Fennel & apple slaw → Pork → Tonkatsu mayo →
Bun top

INSTRUCTIONS

1 For the slaw, mix all the ingredients together in a bowl. Season with salt and freshly ground black pepper.

2 For the pork, cut the loin into thin slices and beat lightly with a mallet, between sheets of plastic wrap. You want the pork to be about 3 mm (⅛ in) thick, and 3 cm x 4 cm (1¼ in x 1½ in) in size.

3 Whisk together the egg and milk. Dredge the pork in the flour, then dip in the egg wash, then the panko crumbs, making sure you press the crumbs into the pork well.

4 To serve, heat a frying pan over a medium heat and add about 5 mm (¼ in) of oil. Allow the oil to heat, then carefully lower the crumbed pork in. Cook for 2–3 minutes, or until golden, then turn over and cook until golden on the other side. Remove from the pan and immediately drain on paper towel. Season with a little salt, then build your burgers.

TONKATSU MAYO

FENNEL & APPLE SLAW

— Fig. 22 —

TURKEY BURGER WITH CRANBERRY MAYO & KALE ^{TU}

When I was living in the United States, I found turkey to be a very popular lean meat option. However, because it's so lean, turkey can dry out quite easily. To combat this I've added a small amount of bacon to these patties, which not only adds moisture, but also imparts a subtle smoky flavour *(see Fig. 23)*.

MAKES 4

400 g (14 oz) minced (ground) turkey	4 soft burger buns (see page 10), cut in half
100 g (3½ oz) minced (ground) or very finely chopped bacon	melted clarified butter (page 117), for brushing
1½ teaspoons sea salt	125 g (4½ oz/½ cup) cranberry mayo (page 124)
½ teaspoon freshly ground black pepper	4 kale leaves, stems removed

BUILD FROM THE BOTTOM, IN THIS ORDER:

Bun bottom → Cranberry mayo → Turkey patty → Kale → Bun top

INSTRUCTIONS

1 Put the turkey and bacon in a large bowl, add the salt and pepper and mix well. Weigh the mixture out into four 125 g (4½ oz) portions and form into patties. Reserve between sheets of baking paper in the fridge until ready to cook.

2 Heat a flat grill plate, or a large non-stick frying pan, to a medium heat. Cook the patties for 4–5 minutes on each side, or until cooked through. Keep in a warm place.

3 Brush the insides of the buns with clarified butter and toast lightly on the grill, then build your burgers.

— Fig. 23 —

HONEY SOY CHICKEN BURGER WITH SESAME SLAW HS

This is my version of a teriyaki burger *(see Fig. 24)*. The sweet and salty flavour of the honey and soy is accented perfectly by the nuttiness of the roasted sesame oil. As the honey can burn easily, the chicken thighs are cooked in the oven; you can chargrill them if you like, but they are prone to stick.

MAKES 4

80 ml (2½ oz/⅓ cup)
  light soy sauce
1 tablespoon honey
4 spring onions (scallions),
  cut into 5 cm (2 in) lengths
1 teaspoon sesame oil
1 tablespoon sesame seeds,
  lightly toasted
4 boneless chicken thighs,
  about 150 g (5½ oz) each,
  skin on
4 soft burger buns (see
  page 10), cut in half
melted clarified butter
  (page 117), for brushing
60 g (2 oz/¼ cup) jalapeño
  & Thai basil mayo
  (page 122)

Sesame slaw
75 g (2¾ oz/1 cup) finely
  shredded cabbage
2 tablespoons coriander
  (cilantro) leaves,
  washed and dried
1 teaspoon rice vinegar
1 tablespoon peanut oil
1 teaspoons sesame oil
1 tablespoons sesame seeds,
  lightly toasted

BUILD FROM THE BOTTOM, IN THIS ORDER:

Bun bottom → Jalapeño & Thai basil mayo → Chicken →
Sesame slaw → Bun top

INSTRUCTIONS

1 In a bowl, combine the soy sauce, honey and spring onion. Stir in the sesame oil and sesame seeds. Add the chicken and mix thoroughly, turning to coat. Cover and marinate in the fridge for at least 2 hours, or overnight.

2 Preheat the oven to 180°C (350°F). Line a roasting tin with foil and add the chicken in a single layer. Bake for 20 minutes, turning and mixing every 5 minutes. Check to see if the chicken is done; if it isn't, continue cooking a little longer.

3 For the slaw, add the cabbage and coriander to a bowl. Add the vinegar, peanut oil, sesame oil and sesame seeds and toss together. When the chicken is out of the oven, pick out the spring onion pieces and toss them through the slaw.

4 To assemble the burgers, heat a flat grill plate, or a non-stick frying pan, to a medium heat. Brush the insides of the buns with clarified butter and toast lightly on the grill, then build your burgers.

JALAPEÑO & THAI
BASIL MAYO

HONEY SOY
CHICKEN

SESAME SLAW

— Fig. 24 —

KARAAGE CHICKEN BURGER WITH
WOMBOK SLAW & PICKLED GINGER MAYO ^{KA}

Here's a deliciously Japanese-style chicken burger, in which the slightly sweet and salty flavour of the sake and soy work perfectly with the crispness of the potato starch and cornflour coating. The wombok slaw brings it all together and adds freshness *(see Fig. 25)*. Enjoy with a cold crisp beer, or even sake.

MAKES 4

vegetable oil, for deep-frying
125 g (4½ oz/1 cup)
    potato starch
125 g (4½ oz/1 cup)
    cornflour (cornstarch)
4 soft burger buns (see
    page 10), cut in half
melted clarified butter
    (page 117), for brushing

Karaage chicken
2 tablespoons shio koji
    (salt-fermented rice)
1 tablespoon sake
1 tablespoon soy sauce
20 g (¾ oz) knob of fresh
    ginger, peeled and grated
4 boneless, skinless chicken
    thighs, 120–150 g
    (4½–5½ oz) each

Pickled ginger mayo
2 tablespoons Japanese pickled
    ginger, plus 1 teaspoon
    of the pickling liquid
1 tablespoon lemon juice
1 tablespoon soy sauce
125 g (4½ oz/½ cup) basic
    mayo (page 120)

Wombok slaw
2 large wombok
    (Chinese cabbage)
    leaves, thinly sliced
1 small carrot, finely julienned
10 cm (4 in) piece of daikon,
    about 4 cm (1½ in) wide,
    peeled and finely julienned
2 spring onions (scallions),
    thinly sliced
4 shiso or coriander (cilantro)
    leaves, thinly sliced
60 g (2 oz/¼ cup) basic mayo
    (page 120)

BUILD FROM THE BOTTOM, IN THIS ORDER:

Bun bottom → Wombok slaw → Chicken → Pickled ginger mayo →
Bun top

INSTRUCTIONS

1 For the karaage chicken, place the shio koji, sake, soy sauce and ginger in a small bowl and mix well. Add the chicken thighs and turn to coat in the marinade. Cover with plastic wrap, then marinate in the fridge for 30 minutes to 1 hour.

2 For the pickled ginger mayo, mix all the ingredients together and reserve in the fridge.

3 For the slaw, place the wombok, carrot, daikon and spring onion into iced water together for about 15 minutes, so they crisp up. Drain, then use a salad spinner to dry them out. Cover and reserve in the fridge.

4 To serve, heat about 10 cm (4 in) of oil in a medium saucepan, to about 175°C (345°F). You can test by dipping a wooden chopstick in – the oil should sizzle when ready.

5 Mix the potato starch and cornflour in a large bowl. Remove the chicken thighs from the marinade and toss them in the mixture until they are dry-ish and well coated.

6 Carefully place two of the chicken thighs into the oil and fry for 5–6 minutes, or until golden, crisp and cooked through. Drain immediately on paper towel and keep warm. Repeat with the remaining chicken.

7 While the chicken is cooking, add the shiso leaves and mayo to the wombok slaw and toss well.

8 To assemble the burgers, heat a flat grill plate, or a non-stick frying pan, to a medium heat. Brush the insides of the buns with clarified butter and toast lightly on the grill. Cut each chicken thigh into 4–5 slices, then build your burgers.

SOFT BURGER BUN

PICKLED GINGER MAYO

KARAAGE CHICKEN

WOMBOK SLAW

— Fig. 25 —

CRUMBED SNAPPER BURGER WITH TARTARE SAUCE ^{SN}

As a kid I was quite fond of a Fillet-o-fish. This is my version, made using real, good-quality fish *(see Fig. 26)*. If you can't get snapper, any firm, sweet white fish, such as cod or even monkfish, would work well.

MAKES 4

2 free-range eggs
100 ml (3½ fl oz) milk
75 g (2¾ oz/½ cup) plain (all-purpose) flour, for dusting
120 g (4½ oz/2 cups) panko (Japanese) breadcrumbs
4 x 100 g (3½ oz) pieces of snapper, skinless and boneless

vegetable oil, for deep-frying
4 soft burger buns (see page 10), cut in half
melted clarified butter (page 117), for brushing
125 g (4½ oz/½ cup) tartare sauce (page 126)
8 butter (bibb) lettuce leaves, washed and dried
2 lemon wedges

BUILD FROM THE BOTTOM, IN THIS ORDER:

Bun bottom → Tartare sauce → Lettuce → Fish fillet → A squeeze of lemon juice → A sprinkling of sea salt → Bun top

INSTRUCTIONS

1 Whisk the eggs and milk together in a bowl. Place the flour and crumbs in two separate bowls. Season the snapper fillets with salt and freshly ground black pepper. Dredge the fish in the flour, then shake off the excess. Dip into the egg wash, then into the panko crumbs. Press lightly to make sure the fish is well coated with the crumbs and there are no gaps in the coating. Reserve in the fridge until ready to fry, but try to coat the fish as close to cooking as possible, so the crumbs don't absorb too much moisture.

2 Heat about 10 cm (4 in) of oil in a medium saucepan, to about 175°C (345°F). You can test by dipping a wooden chopstick in – the oil should sizzle when ready.

3 Carefully lower two of the snapper fillets into the oil and fry for 2–3 minutes, or until golden, crisp and cooked through. Drain immediately on paper towel and keep warm. Repeat with the remaining two fish fillets.

4 Meanwhile, heat a large non-stick frying pan or flat grill plate to a medium heat. Brush the insides of the buns with clarified butter and toast lightly on the grill, then build your burgers.

— Fig. 26 —

CHICKPEA BURGER WITH TAHINI YOGHURT ^{CK}

SOFT BURGER BUN

TAHINI YOGHURT

ROCKET (ARUGULA)

CHICKPEA PATTY

TOMATO KASUNDI

RECIPE PAGE 74

— Fig. 27 —

LOBSTER BURGER WITH TOBIKO AND WASABI & MISO MAYO ^{LO}

SOFT BURGER BUN

LOBSTER TOSSED WITH SPRING ONION, SESAME SEEDS, WAKAME AND WASABI & MISO MAYO

WAKAME

TOBIKO (FLYING FISH ROE)

RECIPE PAGE 75

— Fig. 28 —

CHICKPEA BURGER WITH TAHINI YOGHURT ^{CK}

Here's one for those who appreciate a good vegetarian burger. The falafel-style patty, with the added nutritional bonus of kale, works perfectly with the tahini yoghurt and kasundi, to make a filling yet healthy burger *(see Fig. 27).*

MAKES 4

vegetable oil, for deep-frying
4 soft burger buns (see
    page 10), cut in half
olive oil, for brushing
60 ml (2 fl oz/¼ cup)
    tomato kasundi (page 130)
35 g (1¼ oz/1 cup) rocket
    (arugula) leaves

Tahini yoghurt
125 g (4½ oz/½ cup)
    Greek-style yoghurt
2 tablespoons tahini
2 tablespoons olive oil
1 tablespoon lemon juice
2 tablespoons mint leaves,
    thinly sliced

Chickpea patties
320 g (11½ oz/2 cups)
    cooked chickpeas
2 French shallots, diced
2 garlic cloves, roughly
    chopped
1 tablespoon ground cumin
1 teaspoon ground coriander
½ teaspoon chilli powder
2 tablespoons thinly sliced
    coriander (cilantro) leaves
4 kale leaves, stems removed,
    thinly sliced
30 g (1 oz/¼ cup) besan
    (chickpea flour)

BUILD FROM THE BOTTOM, IN THIS ORDER:

Bun bottom → Tomato kasundi → Chickpea patty → Rocket →
Tahini yoghurt → Bun top

INSTRUCTIONS

1 For the tahini yoghurt, put the yoghurt in a fine-mesh seive set over a bowl. Leave to drain in the fridge overnight. Next day, near serving time, mix the yoghurt with the remaining ingredients and set aside at room temperature.

2 For the patties, place the chickpeas in a food processor with the shallot, garlic and spices. Season with sea salt and freshly ground black pepper and blitz to make a dough. Place in a bowl and fold the coriander leaves, kale and besan through. Form into four evenly sized patties, the circumference of the buns. Reserve between sheets of baking paper in the fridge; the patties can be made up to a day ahead.

3 To serve, heat about 10 cm (4 in) of oil in a large saucepan over a medium–high heat, to 175°C (345°F). You can test by dipping a wooden chopstick in – the oil should sizzle when ready.

4 Carefully lower two patties into the oil and cook for 2 minutes, or until one side is golden. Turn over and cook the other side for about 2 minutes, until golden. Remove with a slotted spoon and immediately drain on paper towel. Repeat with the other two patties.

5 Meanwhile, heat a large non-stick frying pan over a medium heat. Brush the insides of the buns with olive oil and toast lightly in the pan, then build your burgers.

LOBSTER BURGER WITH TOBIKO AND WASABI & MISO MAYO ^{LO}

This is my Japanese-style lobster roll *(see Fig. 28)*. It is based on a classic New England–style lobster roll, but with Japanese flavours. I use claw and knuckle meat from North Atlantic lobster, but you could use just the tail, or buy a whole lobster and pick all the meat out of it.

MAKES 4

400 g (14 oz) lobster claw
and knuckle meat
2 spring onions (scallions),
thinly sliced
40 g (1½ oz/¼ cup) sesame
seeds, lightly toasted
2 tablespoons wakame
seaweed, rehydrated
in water
250 g (9 oz/1 cup) wasabi
& miso mayo (page 123)

4 soft burger buns (see
page 10), cut in half
melted clarified butter
(page 117), for brushing
3 tablespoons orange tobiko
(flying fish roe)

BUILD FROM THE BOTTOM, IN THIS ORDER:

Bun bottom → Lobster mixture → Tobiko → Bun top

INSTRUCTIONS

1 Pick through the lobster meat to make sure there are no bits of shell. Cover and leave on a work surface for 30 minutes, to come to room temperature.

2 Toss the lobster with the spring onion, sesame seeds, wakame and enough of the mayonnaise so the mixture is well coated, but not too soaked.

3 Heat a large non-stick frying pan, or flat grill plate, to a medium heat. Brush the insides of the buns with clarified butter and toast lightly on the grill, then build your burgers.

PRAWN TOGARASHI BURGER WITH YUZU & SESAME MAYO ^{PT}

This is quite a light and refreshing burger *(see Fig. 29)*. If you want to keep the flavours really clean and not so rich, you can leave the bun untoasted.

MAKES 4

12 cooked prawns, peeled and deveined, tails removed
125 g (4½ oz/½ cup) sesame & yuzu mayo (page 121)
4 soft burger buns (see page 10), cut in half
melted clarified butter (page 117), for brushing

1 tablespoon togarashi (Japanese seven-spice pepper)
4 iceberg lettuce leaves, washed, dried and thinly sliced

BUILD FROM THE BOTTOM, IN THIS ORDER:

Bun bottom → Lettuce → Prawns → A sprinkling of togarashi → Bun top

INSTRUCTIONS

1 Toss the prawns with the mayo until well coated.

2 Heat a flat grill plate, or a non-stick frying pan, to a medium heat. Brush the insides of the buns with clarified butter and toast lightly on the grill, then build your burgers.

PRAWNS TOSSED
IN SESAME
& YUZU MAYO

ICEBERG LETTUCE

TOGARASHI

— Fig. 29 —

SOFT-SHELL CRAB BURGER WITH GREEN MANGO SALAD & CHILLI DRESSING ^{CR}

This is what I would call a Thai-style burger *(see Fig. 30)*. It has some lightly fried soft-shell crab, then a crisp, acidic green mango salad with a hot, sweet, salty and sour dressing. Soft-shell crabs are easy eating; they are simply crabs that have recently moulted (shed their hard shells), which they do each spring.

To clean soft-shell crabs, you need to lift up each side of the top shell and remove the filters (long pointy things), cut off the face, and also remove the tail that curls underneath. Be sure to dry them off as thoroughly as possible so they don't spit during frying.

MAKES 4

vegetable oil, for deep-frying
90 g (3 oz/½ cup) rice flour
45 g (1½ oz) potato starch
4 soft-shell crabs, cleaned
4 soft burger buns (see
   page 10), cut in half
melted clarified butter
   (page 117), for brushing

Chilli dressing
1 bird's eye chilli, sliced
1 garlic clove, sliced
25 g (1 oz) palm sugar
   (jaggery), chopped
50 ml (1¾ fl oz) lime juice
50 ml (1¾ fl oz) fish sauce

Green mango salad
2 green mangoes,
   peeled and julienned
1 long red chilli,
   seeded and julienned
2 tablespoons roasted
   peanuts, chopped
8 Thai basil leaves, torn
8 coriander (cilantro)
   leaves, torn

INSTRUCTIONS

1 For the chilli dressing, place the ingredients in a deep container and blitz with a hand-held blender.

2 For the green mango salad, toss the mango with the chilli, peanuts and herbs, and enough of the chilli dressing to coat well.

3 For the crab, heat about 10 cm (4 in) of oil in a medium saucepan, to about 175°C (345°F). You can test by dipping a wooden chopstick in – the oil should sizzle when ready.

4 Mix the rice flour and potato starch in a large bowl. Toss the crabs in the flours until dry-ish and well coated. Carefully place two of the crabs into the oil and fry for 3–4 minutes, or until golden, crisp and cooked through. Drain immediately on paper towel and keep warm. Repeat with the remaining two crabs.

5 Meanwhile, heat a large non-stick frying pan, or flat grill plate, to a medium heat. Brush the insides of the buns with clarified butter and toast lightly on the grill, then build your burgers.

BUILD FROM THE BOTTOM, IN THIS ORDER:

Bun bottom → Green Mango salad → Crab → Bun top

SOFT BURGER BUN

CRISPY-FRIED
SOFT-SHELL CRAB

GREEN MANGO SALAD

— Fig. 30 —

CLAM PO' BOY BURGER WITH JALAPEÑO & THAI BASIL MAYO ^{CM}

Po' boys are originally from New Orleans, and usually feature either prawns (shrimp) or oysters, served in a long white roll. This is a burger version using clams *(see Fig. 31)*. I love their texture and slight saltiness.

MAKES 4

20 clams (vongole), cooked and
    removed from their shells
100 ml (3½ fl oz) buttermilk,
    or 100 ml (3½ fl oz) milk
    with ½ teaspoon lemon
    juice added
vegetable oil, for deep-frying
4 soft burger buns (see
    page 10), cut in half
melted clarified butter
    (page 117), for brushing
4 iceberg lettuce leaves,
    washed, dried and
    thinly sliced
125 g (4½ oz/½ cup)
    jalapeño & Thai basil
    mayo (page 122)

Spiced flour
1 teaspoon cayenne pepper
1 teaspoon ground turmeric
3 teaspoons sweet paprika
2 teaspoons salt
3 teaspoons ground cumin
1 teaspoon Chinese five-spice
3 teaspoons ground coriander
2 teaspoons garlic powder
2 teaspoons onion powder
3 teaspoons ground
    sichuan pepper
2 teaspoons ground
    white pepper
150 g (5½ oz/1 cup) plain
    (all-purpose) flour

BUILD FROM THE BOTTOM, IN THIS ORDER:

Bun bottom → Lettuce → Jalapeño & Thai basil mayo →
Clams → Bun top

INSTRUCTIONS

1 Soak the clams in the buttermilk for about 5 minutes or so, to add a nice flavour and help the flour stick when dredging.

2 For the spiced flour, mix all the ingredients together in a large bowl and set aside.

3 To serve, heat about 10 cm (4 in) of oil in a large saucepan, to about 175°C (345°F). You can test by dipping a wooden chopstick in – the oil should sizzle when ready.

4 Remove the clams from the milk in small batches. Toss well with the spiced flour, then shake off the excess using a sieve. Gently lower the clams into the oil and cook for 2–3 minutes, or until golden and crisp. Drain immediately on paper towel and keep warm. Repeat with the remaining clams.

5 Meanwhile, heat a large non-stick frying pan, or flat grill plate, to a medium heat. Brush the insides of the buns with clarified butter and toast lightly on the grill, then build your burgers.

— Fig. 31 —

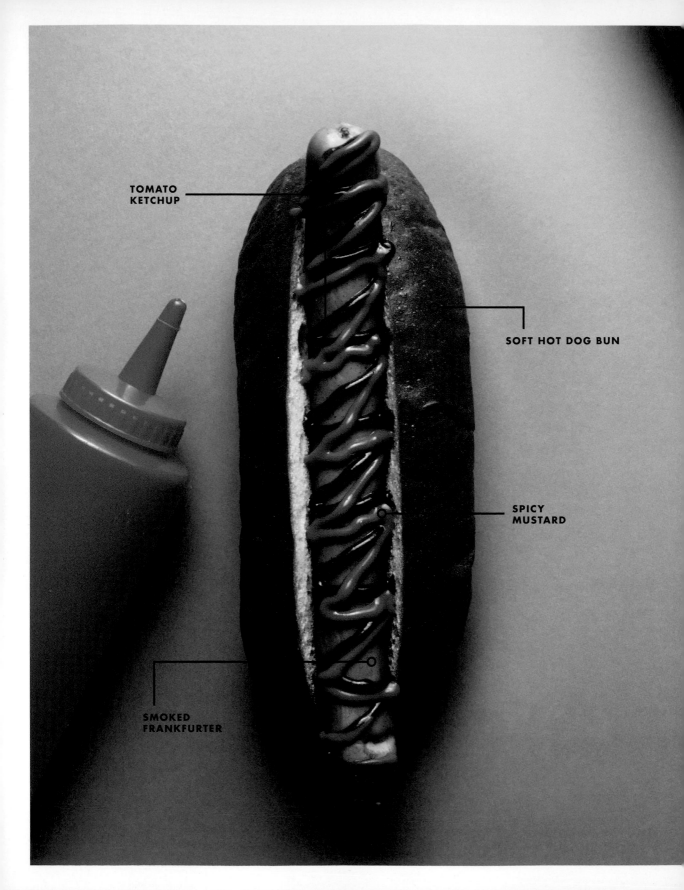

TOMATO
KETCHUP

SOFT HOT DOG BUN

SPICY
MUSTARD

SMOKED
FRANKFURTER

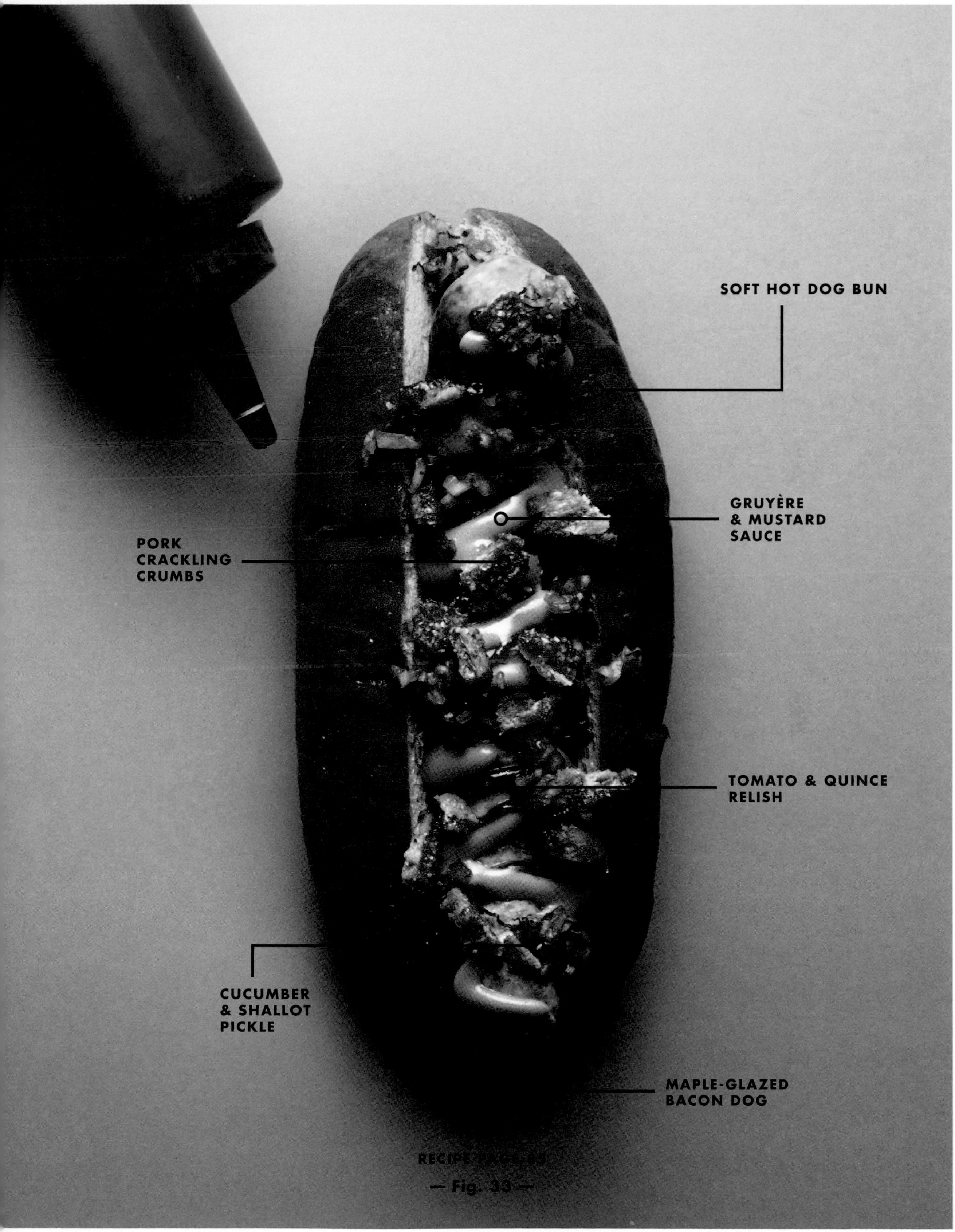

SOFT HOT DOG BUN

GRUYÈRE
& MUSTARD
SAUCE

PORK
CRACKLING
CRUMBS

TOMATO & QUINCE
RELISH

CUCUMBER
& SHALLOT
PICKLE

MAPLE-GLAZED
BACON DOG

RECIPE PAGE 85

— Fig. 33 —

CLASSIC HOT DOG ^{HD}

Like burgers, hot dogs are one of the best 'things in bread' to devour *(see Fig. 32)*. They can easily be eaten with one hand, and you can put whatever you like on them. The most important part is the sausage – traditionally a smoked thin pork or beef emulsified sausage originating from Frankfurt in Germany. They became very popular in the United States around the end of the nineteenth century, and are now synonymous with baseball! The frankfurts are usually either steamed or grilled, and the bun is often steamed to make it very soft. The classic version below features the most commonly used condiments; choose whichever ones you like, in quantities to suit your taste.

MAKES 4

4 quality smoked frankfurters
4 hot dog buns

Other bits
tomato ketchup (page 116)
spicy mustard (page 117)
grated cheese
pickles (page 136)
finely diced onion
basic mayo (page 120)
jalapeño chillies
sauerkraut

BUILD FROM THE BOTTOM, IN THIS ORDER:

Bun → Frankfurter → Other bits!

INSTRUCTIONS

1 Heat the frankfurters in a steamer, or in a frying pan over a medium heat with a little vegetable oil.

2 Heat the buns in a steamer until soft.

3 Open the buns and add the frankfurters. Top with whichever condiments take your fancy...

MAPLE-GLAZED BACON DOG WITH TOMATO & QUINCE RELISH AND MUSTARD PICKLES ^{BD}

This recipe *(see Fig. 33)* was used for a challenge on *MasterChef Australia*. The contestants had two hours to prepare all the elements, including making brioche hot dog rolls from scratch (rest easy, you can just use regular hot dog buns here). It was quite a challenge, and amusing to watch. The assorted condiments all bring different flavours and textures to this amazing dog.

MAKES 8

1 piece of pork skin, about 15 cm (6 in) square, scored lightly at 1 cm (½ in) intervals
olive oil, for pan-frying
8 hot dog buns, split down the middle
tomato & poached quince relish (page 131)
cucumber & shallot pickle (page 137)

Gruyère & mustard sauce
50 ml (1¾ fl oz) thickened (whipping) cream
50 ml (1¾ fl oz) white wine, such as chardonnay
60 g (2 oz/¼ cup) dijon mustard
125 g (4½ oz) gruyère or comté cheese, finely grated

Bacon sausages
100 g (3½ oz) kaiserfleisch (streaky bacon), cut into small chunks
50 ml (1¾ fl oz) maple syrup
250 g (9 oz) minced (ground) veal
250 g (9 oz) minced (ground) pork
100 g (3½ oz) pork back fat, finely diced
25 ml (¾ fl oz) brandy
¼ teaspoon quatre épices ('four-spice' mix of ground cloves, nutmeg, ginger and pepper)
2 teaspoons sea salt
¼ teaspoon freshly ground black pepper
natural sausage casing

BUILD FROM THE BOTTOM, IN THIS ORDER:

Bun → Bacon sausage → Tomato & quince relish → Gruyère & mustard sauce → Cucumber & shallot pickle → Pork crackling crumbs

INSTRUCTIONS

1 Preheat the oven to 180°C (350°F). Season the pork skin well with sea salt. Roast on a baking tray for 30 minutes, or until bubbly and crisp. Leave to cool, then break into pieces. Using a mortar and pestle, pound to the size of cardamom pods.

2 For the sausages, heat a non-stick frying pan over a medium–high heat. Cook the bacon until the fat starts to render, then add the maple syrup and cook for 30 seconds. Transfer to a tray lined with baking paper and chill until cold.

3 Working quickly, place the other sausage ingredients (except the sausage casing) in an electric mixer fitted with a paddle attachment, set to medium speed. Add the cold bacon and mix to a well-combined, sticky paste (about 2 minutes); the mixture must be as cold as possible to combine properly. Transfer to a bowl, cover with plastic wrap and refrigerate until cold.

4 Using a piping (icing) bag, place the tube about 3 cm (1¼ in) into the sausage casing, then feed the meat mixture through, filling to the desired width. Tie into sausages, then chill for 5 minutes. Meanwhile, set a pot of water over a medium–low heat and bring to a poaching temperature (60°C/140°F; there should be no movement in the water). Poach the sausages for 8 minutes, then remove and cool on a tray.

5 For the gruyère sauce, gently warm the cream and wine in a saucepan. Whisk in the mustard, then the cheese, taking care not to overheat. Season with black pepper and keep in a warm place.

6 Heat some olive oil in a non-stick frying pan over a medium heat. Lightly prick the sausages with a fork. Cook for 3–4 minutes, turning, until golden and heated through, then assemble your hot dogs.

PEPPERED STEAK BURGER WITH CARAMELISED ONION & HORSERADISH CREAM ^{PS}

This is a bit of a fancy burger. The peppery charred flavour of the steak is offset by the sweetness of the caramelised onions and the tangy sharpness of the horseradish cream. The runny egg yolk just brings it all together perfectly *(see Fig. 34)*.

MAKES 4

4 x 120 g (4½ oz) beef
  eye fillets, butterflied
freshly cracked black pepper,
  for seasoning
olive oil, for drizzling
  and pan-frying
4 free-range eggs
4 soft burger buns (see
  page 10), cut in half
melted clarified butter
  (page 117), for brushing
1 quantity caramelised onion
  (page 127)
100 g (3½ oz) rocket
  (arugula) leaves

Horseradish cream
125 g (4½ oz/½ cup) crème
  fraîche or sour cream
2 tablespoons fresh grated
  horseradish, or bottled
  horseradish sauce
juice of 1 lemon

BUILD FROM THE BOTTOM, IN THIS ORDER:

Bun bottom → Caramelised onion → Steak → Egg → Rocket →
Bun top, generously spread with horseradish cream

INSTRUCTIONS

1 For the horseradish cream, place all the ingredients in a bowl and whisk together, to the consistency of firmly whipped cream. Be careful not to let the crème fraîche get too warm or it will not whip properly. Season with salt and freshly ground black pepper. Cover and reserve in the fridge.

2 Heat a cast-iron grill pan, or barbecue, to a high heat. Heat a large non-stick frying pan over a medium heat.

3 Generously season the steaks on both sides with sea salt and cracked black pepper, then lightly drizzle with olive oil. Cook on the grill for about 1 minute on each side for medium-rare. Rest the steaks on a rack for a minute.

4 Meanwhile, add a little olive oil to the hot frying pan. Add the eggs and fry for about 2 minutes, until they have reached the sunny-side-up stage.

5 While the steaks are resting, brush the insides of the buns with clarified butter and toast lightly on the grill, until light char marks appear. Now build your burgers.

FRIED FREE-RANGE EGG

ROCKET (ARUGULA)

EYE-FILLET STEAK
GENEROUSLY
SEASONED WITH
PEPPER

HORSERADISH
CREAM

— Fig. 34 —

THE REUBEN BURGER ^{RE}

I fell in love with Reubens when I was living in Michigan… but then when I lived in New York, I was a stone's throw from Katz's Deli – the home of the mother of all Reubens! This one is a little lighter on the meat than theirs. She's a saucy one, but also super tasty *(see Fig. 35)*.

MAKES 4

2 tablespoons vegetable oil
600 g (1 lb 5 oz) thinly
   sliced corned beef
150 g (5½ oz/1 cup)
   sauerkraut, drained
   of excess juice
8 slices Swiss cheese

4 soft burger buns (see
   page 10), cut in half
melted clarified butter
   (page 117), for brushing
250 ml (8½ fl oz/1 cup)
   thousand island dressing
   (page 125)

BUILD FROM THE BOTTOM, IN THIS ORDER:

Bun bottom → Thousand island dressing → Corned beef, Swiss cheese & sauerkraut stack → Thousand island dressing → Bun top

INSTRUCTIONS

1 Preheat the oven to 175°C (345°F). Line a baking tray with baking paper.

2 Heat a flat grill plate, or a large non-stick frying pan, to a medium heat. Add the oil, then gently cook the corned beef until it is warmed through.

3 Meanwhile, place the sauerkraut in a small saucepan and warm it through.

4 Separate the warmed corned beef into four equal piles, about the same circumference as the buns. Place a slice of cheese on top of each mound, top with the sauerkraut, then top each with another slice of cheese. Place the tray in the oven for 3–4 minutes, or until the cheese has melted.

5 While the beef is in the oven, brush the insides of the buns with clarified butter and toast lightly on the grill, then build your burgers.

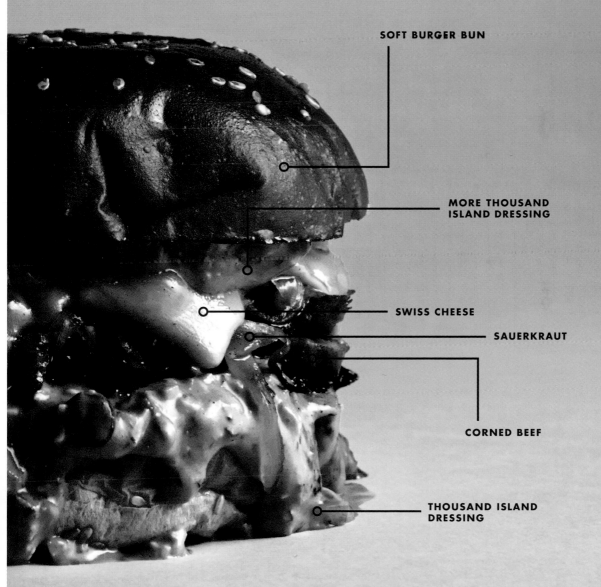

SOFT BURGER BUN

MORE THOUSAND
ISLAND DRESSING

SWISS CHEESE

SAUERKRAUT

CORNED BEEF

THOUSAND ISLAND
DRESSING

— Fig. 35 —

DOUCHE BURGER ^{DO}

This burger was created as an icon dish for the Taste of Melbourne food and wine festival in 2013. Much like the 'yuppies' of the 1980s, this burger is based on excess. That's why we called it such an unsavoury name – it is all about showing off. However, the burger itself is bloody delicious! Because it is so rich, it is best served on mini burger buns *(see Fig. 36)*.

MAKES 4

4 x 80 g (2¾ oz) slices of wagyu eye fillet, about 5 mm (¼ in) thick

4 x 40 g (1½ oz) slices foie gras, about 5 mm (¼ in) thick

4 soft mini burger buns (see page 10), cut in half

melted clarified butter (page 117), for brushing

60 ml (2 fl oz/¼ cup) cherry ketchup (page 116)

60 g (2 oz/¼ cup) green peppercorn mayo (page 122)

BUILD FROM THE BOTTOM, IN THIS ORDER:

Bun bottom → Cherry ketchup → Steak → Foie gras → Green peppercorn mayo → Bun top

INSTRUCTIONS

1 Heat a non-stick frying pan, or flat grill plate, to a high heat. Season the steak and foie gras well with salt and freshly ground black pepper.

2 Cook both the steak and the foie gras in the hot pan for about 30 seconds on each side. Remove and place somewhere warm to rest.

3 Meanwhile, wipe the pan and heat to a medium heat. Brush the insides of the buns with clarified butter and toast lightly, then build your burgers.

SOFT BURGER BUN

GREEN
PEPPERCORN
MAYO

FOIE GRAS

WAGYU BEEF
EYE FILLET

CHERRY KETCHUP

— Fig. 36 —

THE 'WHICH BEER?' PROJECT ^{WB}

(1) The carbonation in beer is great for cutting through the fat in a burger.

(2) Smoky, malty dark beers are the perfect pairing for anything with barbecue sauce.

③ Try a saison to complement the earthy notes in cheese, mustard and onions.

④ Remember, there's nothing wrong with going for your old favourites.

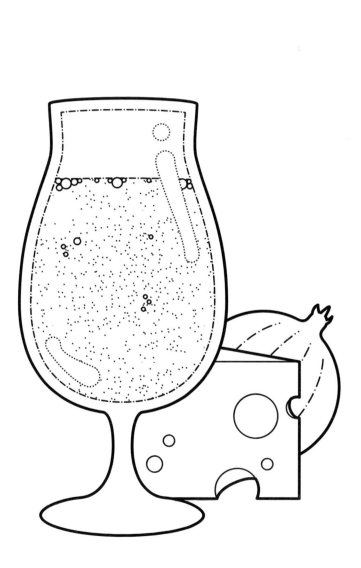

THE 'WHICH BEER?' PROJECT ^{WB}

Which beer is best suited to burgers?

Burgers can become complicated, often crowded by condiments, herbs, various cheeses, and often a chilli kick. This offers up myriad beer-pairing possibilities – as well as a few obstacles to navigate.

We could all find ways to pair our everyday 'go to' beer to any burger, but with craft beers on the rise and enthusiasts looking for a deeper relationship between the two, let's have some fun with it.

Beer has indicative traits that make it the perfect accompaniment for a juicy burger; the rest comes down to personal taste.

Here are some gentle suggestions.

CUTTING THROUGH THE FAT

A beer's best attributes when cutting through fat are its carbonation and bitterness. Steer away from low-fizz styles and beers that are too sweet.

Carbonation does vary within generic styles, but personally, I'd be blowing the froth off German pilsners, golden ales, pales and IPAs (India pale ales).

PAIRING WITH CARAMELISATION AND BARBECUE SAUCE

'Welcome to the dark side.' Caramelisation is the result of perfectly grilling or roasting meat. It tastes awesome and makes people happy.

Barbecue sauce can range between sweet fructose styles to seriously smoky, hot and delicious styles.

When pairing with these, I would go for light-bodied, roasty dark beers – something that leans towards smoky notes and has hints of molasses, while maintaining assertive malt characters.

Brown ales and porters will sit comfortably in this pocket. Yum.

PAIRING WITH EARTHY NOTES

Earthy notes will come from cheese, mustard, onions…
and for you umami heads out there, mushrooms!

These characters play into styles using English malts,
brown ales and even saisons. The IPAs also tick the
boxes with their broad mid-range flavour profiles.

BE YOUR OWN BOSS

Do you want to experiment with something new?
Or do you want what you know you're going
to love?

Sometimes, just drinking beer you like is the right
beer for you – no shame in that.

If you're a lager drinker and you did have an
inclination to drift to new flavour territory, I might
suggest moving onto German kölsch, American
pales, English pales or IPAs.

These will bring some more pronounced hoppy
notes and bitterness to your flavour arsenal,
as well as exploring some fantastic aromatics
and malty good-times.

When you find a style you love, explore expressions
within that style. You'll be surprised just how spoilt
for choice we are these days.

MY TOP PICK

IPA – I think I love you!

A burger has a lot going on, and so does an IPA.
It has the hoppy grunt to stand up to the meat patty,
and enough bitterness and carbonation to get your
mouth ready for another bite.

TO CONCLUDE

Eat more burgers and drink more beer.

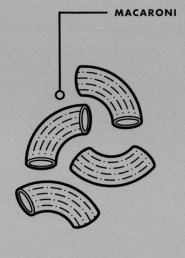

MACARONI

CHIPS

ON THE SIDE

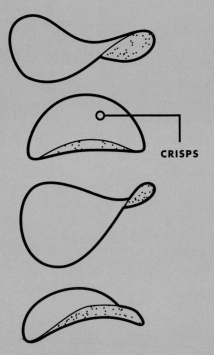

CRISPS

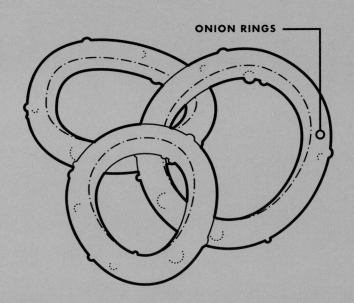

ONION RINGS

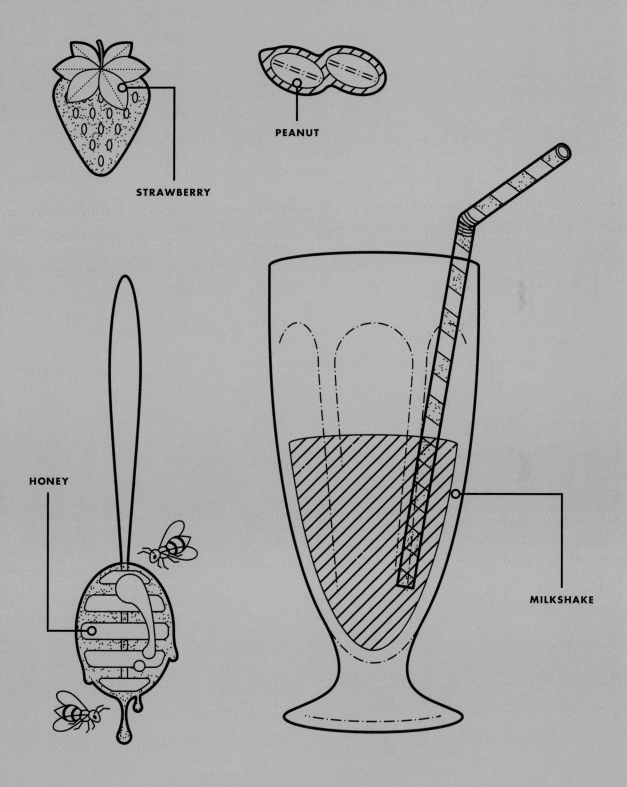

STRAWBERRY

PEANUT

HONEY

MILKSHAKE

HAND-CUT CHIPS ^{HC}

One particular potato reigns supreme
when it comes to chips: the russet burbank,
commonly known as the Idaho potato.
It has a dry, mealy texture, so it has a crisp
exterior and a very light, fluffy interior
when roasted or fried *(see Fig. 37)*. It also
mashes well.

SERVES 4

4 russet burbank potatoes,
    scrubbed and patted
    dry with paper towel
vegetable oil, for deep-frying

INSTRUCTIONS

1 Cook the potatoes at a simmer in a saucepan full
of salted water until tender – about 20–30 minutes,
depending on their size. Drain and leave to cool.

2 Cut the cooled potatoes to your preferred size,
separating the chips so that they don't stick to each
other during cooking. (They can be pre-cooked
a day or two ahead.)

3 In a medium saucepan, heat 10 cm (4 in) of oil to
175°C (345°F). You can test by dipping a wooden
chopstick in – the oil should sizzle when ready.

4 Gently place some of the chips into the oil and
fry for 3–4 minutes, or until golden, crisp and
cooked through. Remove with a slotted spoon
and immediately drain on paper towel. Keep
warm in a low oven until all the chips are done.

5 Season with sea salt and enjoy with your
favourite burger and an ice-cold beer!

— Fig. 37 —

ONION RINGS

As far as I'm concerned, onion rings should have a light, crispy batter and nicely cooked sweet onion inside. These ones *(see Fig. 38)* are made with a fail-safe beer batter, which gives a lovely yeasty flavour.

MAKES 1 MEDIUM BOWL TO SHARE

vegetable oil, for deep-frying
75 g (2¾ oz/½ cup) plain
   (all-purpose) flour,
   for dusting
2 large brown onions, cut into
   slices 1 cm (½ in) thick and
   separated into individual
   rings
sea salt, for sprinkling

Beer batter
110 g (4 oz/¾ cup)
   self-raising flour
30 g (1 oz/¼ cup) cornflour
   (cornstarch)
pinch of sea salt
330 ml (11 fl oz) beer
soda water (club soda)
   as needed

INSTRUCTIONS

1 To make the batter, place the dry ingredients in a bowl, then pour in the beer. Add a little soda water and whisk until just combined. Be careful not to overmix the batter, or it will not be light. Add a little more soda water if needed – the batter should be the consistency of pouring cream.

2 Cover the batter and allow to rest for 30 minutes before using.

3 In a medium saucepan, heat 10 cm (4 in) of oil to 175°C (345°F). You can test by dipping a wooden chopstick in – the oil should sizzle when ready.

4 In a large bowl, mix the flour with a little salt and freshly ground black pepper. Toss the onion rings in the flour until well coated, shaking off the excess.

5 Gently place some of the onion rings into the oil and cook for 1–2 minutes, or until golden. Turn them over and cook for 1–2 minutes on the other side, until crisp and cooked through. Immediately drain on paper towel and repeat with the remaining onion rings.

6 Sprinkle with sea salt and enjoy with your favourite burger and an icy beer.

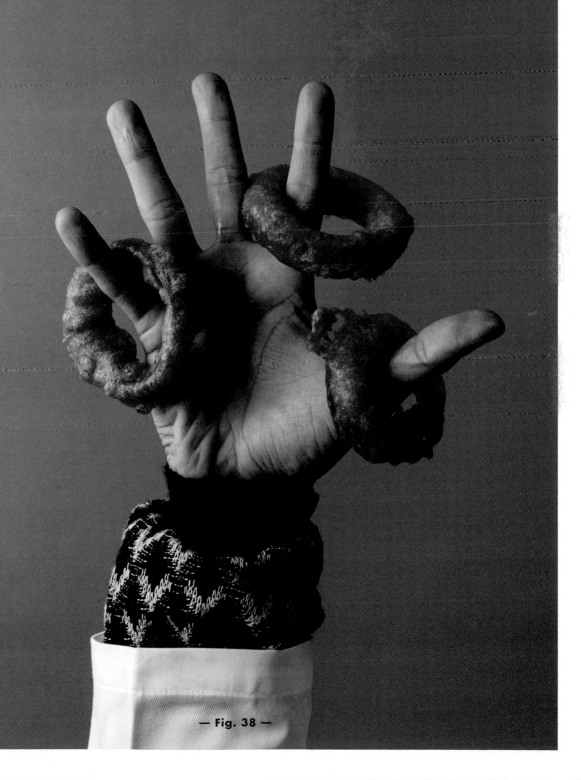

— Fig. 38 —

BAKED MACARONI WITH THREE CHEESES ^{MC}

Macaroni cheese *(see Fig. 39)* is such a crowd pleaser, and here's a nice one to serve alongside some tasty burgers.

SERVES 4 AS PART OF A SHARED MEAL

250 g (9 oz) macaroni
1 bunch chives, thinly sliced
200 g (7 oz) scamorza
    (smoked mozzarella), cut
    into 1 cm (½ in) cubes
75 g (2¾ oz/½ cup) grated
    pepper jack cheese

Béchamel sauce
25 g (1 oz) butter
25 g (1 oz) plain
    (all-purpose) flour
500 ml (17 fl oz/2 cups) milk
100 g (3½ oz) cheddar, grated

INSTRUCTIONS

1 For the béchamel sauce, melt the butter in a saucepan over a medium heat. Add the flour and cook until it just begins to smell nutty, but has no colour.

2 Add the milk and cook, stirring constantly, until it begins to boil. Now turn the heat down and simmer for 5–10 minutes, or until the flour is cooked out and the liquid has thickened a little. Be careful not to burn the bottom of the pan, so keep stirring. Stir in the cheese and season with sea salt and freshly ground black pepper.

3 Meanwhile, bring a large pot of salted water to the boil. Add the pasta, stir well, and cook according to the packet instructions.

4 Once the pasta is just al dente, drain well in a colander. Let sit for 10 minutes for all the water to drain off.

5 To finish, preheat the oven to 175°C (345°F). Place the macaroni in a bowl and pour the béchamel sauce over. Toss the chives and mozzarella through, then transfer to an appropriately sized baking dish. Top with the grated pepper jack cheese.

6 Bake for about 30 minutes, until the sides are bubbling and the cheese on top is golden.

— Fig. 39 —

POTATO CRISPS ^{PC}

A lighter option to have with burgers, these potato crisps go really well with seafood burgers, such as the lobster burger (page 75) or prawn burger (page 76), and are best eaten fresh.

Use potatoes that are not too starchy, as the starch can make the chips turn too dark without becoming crisp. Nicola, king edward and desiree are good all-round choices.

MAKES 1 MEDIUM BOWL TO SHARE

2 large potatoes, scrubbed but not peeled

vegetable oil, for deep-frying
sea salt, for sprinkling

INSTRUCTIONS

1 Using a mandoline, thinly slice the potatoes across their biggest side, to create the largest crisps. Immediately place in cold water to wash off the excess starch and stop browning.

2 In a medium saucepan, heat 10 cm (4 in) of oil to 175°C (345°F). You can test by dipping a wooden chopstick in – the oil should sizzle when ready.

3 Remove the potato slices from the water, then place between sheets of paper towel to absorb the excess moisture. Carefully drop a few slices at a time into the oil, so they cook evenly and don't stick together. Cook for 1–2 minutes, or until golden and crisp – you may need to stir and turn them. Immediately drain on paper towel and repeat with remaining potato slices.

4 Sprinkle with sea salt and crunch away.

MILKSHAKES ^{MS}

At our restaurant, we make some pretty mean shakes *(see Fig. 40)*. Keeping in line with our philosophy of using the best ingredients we can, we also make all of our own flavouring syrups for the shakes.

BASIC MILKSHAKE

MAKES 1

220 ml (7½ fl oz) milk
150 g (5½ oz) quality
    ice cream (3 good scoops)
60 ml (2 fl oz/½ cup)
    syrup of your choice

INSTRUCTIONS

1 Place all the ingredients in a milkshake cup, then place on the milkshake machine for 2–3 minutes, until well mixed and fluffy.

2 If you don't have a milkshake machine, you can use a hand-held blender.

STRAWBERRY SYRUP

MAKES ABOUT 375 ML (12½ FL OZ/1½ CUPS)

500 g (1 lb 2 oz/3⅓ cups)
    fresh strawberries, washed,
    hulled and cut in half
200 g (7 oz) caster
    (superfine) sugar
juice of 2 lemons

INSTRUCTIONS

1 Put the strawberries in a small saucepan with the sugar and lemon juice. Bring to a simmer over a medium heat and cook for 5 minutes. Skim off any scum that collects on top.

2 Let cool slightly, then transfer to a deep container. Blitz with a hand-held blender and let cool.

3 Transfer to an airtight container and keep in the fridge for up to 2 weeks.

MILKSHAKES ^{MS}

PEANUT BUTTER SYRUP

MAKES ABOUT 500 ML (17 FL OZ/2 CUPS)

125 ml (4 fl oz/½ cup) water
250 g (9 oz) caster
   (superfine) sugar

140 g (5 oz/1 cup)
   roasted unsalted peanuts,
   finely ground
pinch of sea salt

INSTRUCTIONS

1 Bring the water and sugar to the boil in a small saucepan, to dissolve the sugar. Allow to cool in a deep container, then add the ground peanuts and salt.

2 Blitz to a smooth syrup, using a hand-held stick blender.

3 Transfer to an airtight container and store at room temperature for up to 2 weeks.

VANILLA SYRUP

MAKES ABOUT 250 ML (8½ FL OZ/1 CUP)

125 ml (4 fl oz/½ cup) water
230 g (8 oz/1 cup) caster
   (superfine) sugar

1 tablespoon vanilla paste
   (we use Heilala vanilla,
   from the Kingdom of Tonga)

INSTRUCTIONS

1 Bring the water and sugar to the boil in a small saucepan to dissolve the sugar. Allow to cool.

2 Add the vanilla paste and whisk well.

3 Keep in an airtight container in the fridge for up to 1 month. Before using, be sure to stir well or shake to redistribute all the vanilla seeds.

CHOCOLATE SYRUP

MAKES ABOUT 250 ML (8½ FL OZ/1 CUP)

250 ml (8½ fl oz/1 cup) water
½ tablespoon liquid glucose

90 g (3 oz/¾ cup)
Dutch (unsweetened)
cocoa powder

INSTRUCTIONS

1 Place the water and glucose in a small saucepan and bring to simmering point.

2 Sift the cocoa powder onto a piece of baking paper.

3 When the water and glucose mixture is simmering, slowly whisk in the cocoa powder until fully combined. Turn the heat down to medium and cook for 5–7 minutes, or until the syrup has thickened and does not taste floury.

4 Strain through a fine sieve to remove any cocoa lumps. Transfer to an airtight container and keep in the fridge for up to 1 month.

BACON MAPLE SYRUP

MAKES ABOUT 250 ML (8½ FL OZ/1 CUP)

4 bacon rashers (slices)
250 ml (8½ fl oz/1 cup)
    maple syrup

125 ml (4 fl oz/½ cup) water
pinch of sea salt

INSTRUCTIONS

1 Heat a grill pan, or non-stick frying pan, over a medium heat. Cook the bacon until crisp, then drain well on paper towel. Break the bacon into small pieces.

2 Put the bacon in a small saucepan with the maple syrup, water and salt. Bring to the boil, then turn the heat down. Simmer until the liquid has reduced by one-third, or back to the original thickness of the maple syrup.

3 Let cool, then blitz with a hand-held blender. Transfer to an airtight container and keep in the fridge for up to 2 weeks.

MILKSHAKES

CHOCOLATE HONEYCOMB SYRUP

MAKES ABOUT 250 ML (8½ FL OZ/1 CUP)

200 g (7 oz) caster
   (superfine) sugar
2 teaspoons liquid glucose
60 ml (2 fl oz/¼ cup)
   water, approximately

3 teaspoons bicarbonate
   of soda (baking soda)
1 quantity chocolate syrup
   (page 107)

INSTRUCTIONS

1 For the honeycomb, put the sugar and glucose in a saucepan, with enough of the water to make a wet 'sand' mixture. Brush down the side of the pan with water, to ensure no sugar crystallises during cooking.

2 Line a tray with baking paper, ready to pour the honeycomb onto. Make sure the tray is sitting on top of a chopping board or the stove, as the honeycomb will be very hot, and the heat can transfer through the tray to the work surface underneath.

3 Put the wet sugar mixture over a high heat and cook for 5–10 minutes, or until the caramel has a very light colour.

4 Now add the bicarbonate of soda and whisk quickly to dissolve. The honeycomb will quickly expand and will keep cooking. As soon as it is slightly paler than the desired colour, pour it onto the baking paper and let it settle. Try not to touch it with the whisk or a spatula once it has been poured, as you will break the bubbles of the honeycomb structure. Allow the honeycomb to completely cool and firm up.

5 Transfer to an airtight container and keep in the fridge for up to 1 month. (You may not need all the honeycomb, but I'm sure you won't have a problem figuring out what to do with the rest!)

6 To make the syrup, take the chocolate syrup and blitz the honeycomb into it, to suit your taste.

SALTED CARAMEL SYRUP

MAKES ABOUT 250 ML (8½ FL OZ/1 CUP)

200 g (7 oz) caster
(superfine) sugar
1 heaped teaspoon
liquid glucose
60 ml (2 fl oz/¼ cup)
water, approximately

200 ml (7 fl oz) thickened
(whipping) cream
½ teaspoon sea salt
80 g (2¾ oz) diced cold butter

INSTRUCTIONS

1 Put the sugar and glucose in a saucepan, with enough of the water to make a wet 'sand' mixture. Brush down the side of the pan with water, to ensure no sugar crystallises during cooking.

2 In a separate saucepan, warm the cream and salt over a medium heat, to just below boiling point.

3 While the cream is coming to the right temperature, put the wet sugar mixture over a high heat and cook for 5–10 minutes, or until a golden caramel colour.

4 Take the caramel off the heat and slowly add in the warmed cream, a little at a time – the mixture spits and boils vigorously, so be careful of splatters as they are hot and will burn you. Once all the cream has been added, let cool for 2 minutes.

5 Now slowly add in the diced cold butter by whisking it in vigorously. Let cool and reserve in an airtight container in the fridge. It will keep for several weeks.

6 Remove from the fridge before using to let the caramel soften again.

STRAWBERRY
SYRUP

BASIC MILKSHAKE

— Fig. 40 —

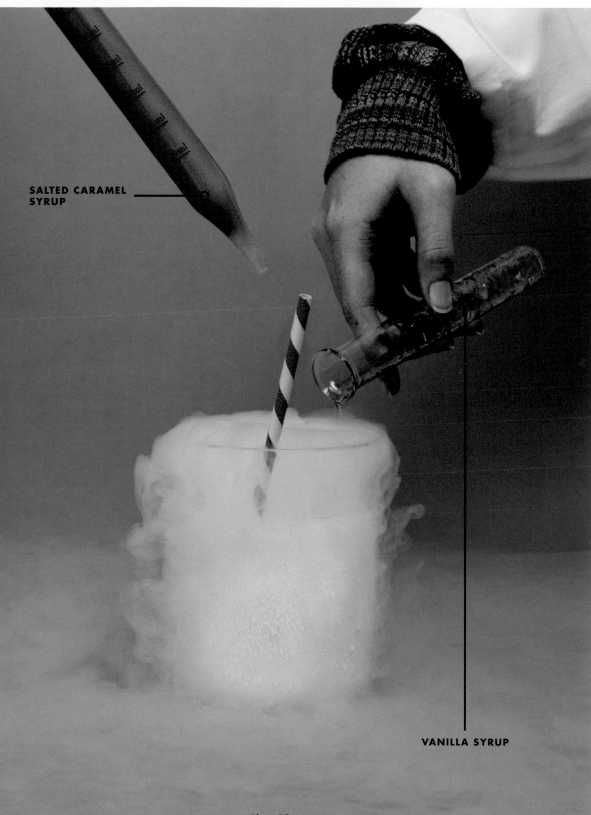

SALTED CARAMEL
SYRUP

VANILLA SYRUP

— Fig. 40 —

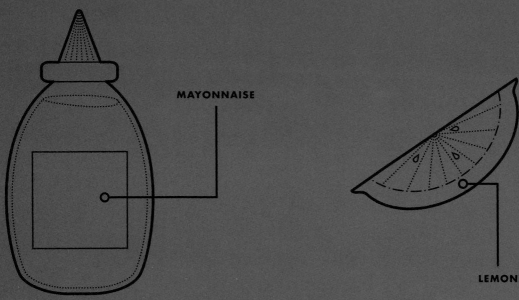

MAYONNAISE

LEMON

ALL THE OTHER BITS

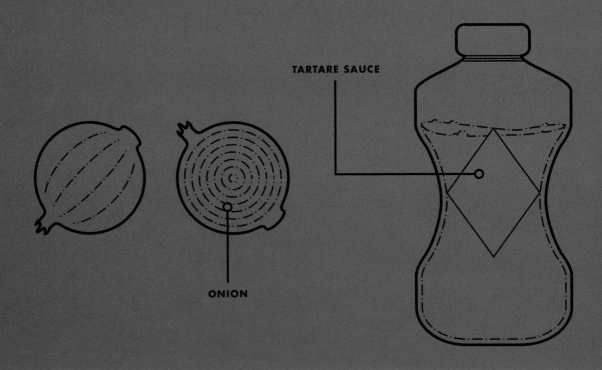

TARTARE SAUCE

ONION

JALAPEÑO

MUSTARD

EGG

TOMATO
KETCHUP

BARBECUE
SAUCE

SOFT BURGER BUNS ^{BB}

These buns are soft and slightly sweet, and simple and quick to make. Also, they compress nicely to hold all of the ingredients in, so the whole burger experience is not too 'bready'.

MAKES 8 BUNS

7 g (¼ oz) dried active yeast
30 g (1 oz) unsalted butter,
   at room temperature
1 free-range egg
430 g (15 oz) plain
   (all-purpose) flour
50 g (1¾ oz) caster
   (superfine) sugar

1 teaspoon sea salt
1 egg yolk, mixed with
   1 tablespoon water
lightly toasted sesame seeds,
   for sprinkling

INSTRUCTIONS

1 Sprinkle the yeast into 250 ml (8½ fl oz/1 cup) lukewarm water and leave for 5–10 minutes, until frothy. Stir to dissolve.

2 In a big bowl, combine the butter, egg, flour, sugar and salt. Add the yeast mixture and mix well, either with your hands, or using an electric mixer with a dough-hook attachment.

3 Turn the dough out onto a lightly floured work surface and knead for about 10 minutes, until you have a soft, smooth dough.

4 Place the dough in a clean, lightly greased bowl. Cover with a tea towel (dish towel) and leave to rise in a warmish place for 1–1½ hours, or until doubled in size.

5 Divide the dough into eight portions and shape each piece into a flattened ball. Place the buns on two greased baking trays, cover with a tea towel and leave to rise for another 30–40 minutes, until they're quite puffy and doubled in size.

6 Meanwhile, preheat the oven to 190°C (375°F).

7 Brush the buns with the egg yolk mixture, then sprinkle with sesame seeds. Bake for 12–15 minutes, or until golden brown.

8 Remove from the oven and leave to cool on a wire rack. Use within 2 days, or freeze for later use. To freeze them, put them in freezer bags, expel as much air as possible and seal tightly; they will keep for several months.

BARBECUE SAUCE ^{BQ}

This sauce *(see Fig. 41)* makes the double cheeseburger with bacon what it is, and is also used for mixing through the pulled pork burger on page 58.

MAKES ABOUT 500 ML (17 FL OZ/2 CUPS)

50 ml (1¾ fl oz) vegetable oil
½ onion, finely diced
1 tablespoon crushed
    fresh garlic
125 ml (4 fl oz/½ cup)
    malt vinegar
125 ml (4 fl oz/½ cup)
    worcestershire sauce
1 tablespoon mustard powder

2 tablespoons dark
    brown sugar
2 tablespoons sweet paprika
1 tablespoon salt
2 tablespoons chipotle
    chilli powder
250 ml (8½ fl oz/1 cup)
    tomato sauce (ketchup)

INSTRUCTIONS

1 Heat a saucepan over a medium heat. Add the oil, then sweat the onion and garlic for about 4 minutes, or until translucent but not coloured.

2 Stir in all the remaining ingredients, except the tomato sauce. Simmer over a medium–low heat for about 15 minutes, or until the sauce has thickened slightly.

3 Add the tomato sauce and cook for 5–10 minutes, or until a sauce-like consistency is reached. Make sure you stir frequently so the sauce doesn't catch.

4 Leave to cool, then blend using an upright blender or hand-held blender. Store in an airtight container in the fridge for up to 1 month.

TOMATO KETCHUP TK

Here is a recipe that I've used a few times, and it will get you something close to the classic old Heinz number *(see Fig. 41)*.

MAKES ABOUT 250 ML (8½ FL OZ/1 CUP)

185 g (6½ oz/¾ cup) tomato paste (concentrated purée)
125 ml (4 fl oz/½ cup) white vinegar
125 ml (4 fl oz/½ cup) light corn syrup

1 tablespoon caster (superfine) sugar
1 teaspoon salt
¼ teaspoon onion powder
⅛ teaspoon garlic powder

INSTRUCTIONS

1 Combine all the ingredients in a non-reactive saucepan. Add 60 ml (2 fl oz/¼ cup) water and whisk over a medium heat until smooth.

2 Bring to the boil, then turn the heat down to a simmer and cook for about 20 minutes, stirring frequently.

3 Once the desired consistency has been reached, remove from the heat and allow to cool.

4 Store in an airtight container in the fridge for up to 1 month.

CHERRY KETCHUP CK

Cherries are such a luxurious fruit, perfectly suited to a ketchup. This one *(see Fig. 41)* goes amazingly well with foie gras.

MAKES ABOUT 250 ML (8½ FL OZ/1 CUP)

100 g (3½ oz) drained tinned cherries
125 g (4½ oz) whole peeled tomatoes
95 g (3¼ oz/½ cup) light brown sugar

125 ml (4 fl oz/½ cup) malt vinegar
1 cinnamon stick
2 star anise

INSTRUCTIONS

1 Place all the ingredients in a non-reactive saucepan and cook over a medium heat for 10–15 minutes, or until the mixture starts to thicken slightly.

2 Remove the spices, then purée to a ketchup consistency using a hand-held blender. Season to taste with salt and allow to cool.

3 Store in an airtight container in the fridge for up to 1 month.

SPICY MUSTARD ^{SM}

This may surprise you, but mustard *(see Fig. 41)* is actually very easy to make. This is a good base recipe that you can personalise to your taste by adding any spices or herbs you like.

MAKES ABOUT 250 G (9 OZ/1 CUP)

2 tablespoons brown
    mustard seeds
2 tablespoons yellow
    mustard seeds

50 ml (1¾ fl oz) port
100 ml (3½ fl oz) red
    wine vinegar
1 tablespoon sugar

INSTRUCTIONS

1 Bring all the ingredients to the boil in a small saucepan. Remove from the heat, cover and let sit at room temperature overnight.

2 Using an upright blender or hand-held blender, blitz to make a seeded mustard. Season with salt and freshly ground black pepper.

3 Keep in an airtight container in the fridge for up to 2 months.

CLARIFIED BUTTER ^{CB}

Clarifying butter is a very simple process. All you are doing is melting the butter and then pouring off the frothy milk solids, leaving a lovely golden fat. Clarified butter lasts longer than regular butter, and can be cooked at a higher temperature without burning. It is also known as ghee.

MAKES ABOUT 375 G (13 OZ/1½ CUPS)

500 g (1 lb 2 oz) butter

INSTRUCTIONS

1 Place the butter in a saucepan over a medium–low heat. Once it has melted, turn the heat down to low.

2 Skim off any scum that rises to the top. Do not stir the butter, but allow the milk solids to catch on the bottom. The liquid will evaporate eventually, and you'll be left with beautiful golden pure clarified butter. Be careful not to let the solids brown, as they will caramelise and turn the mixture into browned butter.

3 Strain through a fine sieve, into an airtight container. Keep in the fridge for up to 1 month.

BASIC MAYONAISSE

TOMATO KETCHUP

— Fig. 41 —

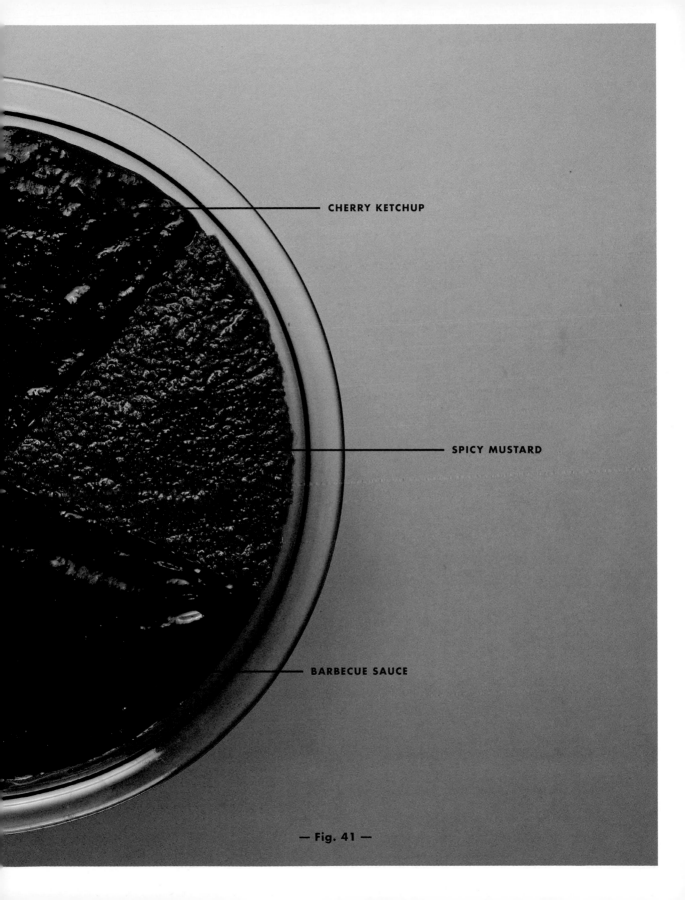

CHERRY KETCHUP

SPICY MUSTARD

BARBECUE SAUCE

— Fig. 41 —

MAYONNAISE ^{MN}

Making mayonnaise *(see Fig. 41)* at home really is incredibly simple, and you'll know exactly what has gone into it.

In our mayo we use only free-range eggs from a farmer in Victoria's Yarra Valley; please always buy the best and most ethically laid eggs you can. Never use extra virgin olive oil in your mayo as it is too strongly flavoured and can also be quite bitter. I'd recommend a fairly neutral vegetable oil; we use a blend of canola and olive oil.

BASIC MAYO

MAKES ABOUT 750 G (1 LB 11 OZ/3 CUPS)

6 egg yolks
50 ml (1¾ fl oz) white
   wine vinegar
60 g (2 oz/¼ cup)
   dijon mustard

2 teaspoons sea salt
2 cups (17 fl oz/500 ml)
   vegetable oil
50 ml (1¾ fl oz) warm water

INSTRUCTIONS

1 Place the egg yolks, vinegar, mustard and salt in a stainless steel or glass bowl, or the bowl of an electric stand mixer. Whisk together to combine.

2 Slowly drizzle the oil down the side of the bowl while whisking constantly. If the mixture becomes too thick, add a little of the warm water to thin it down as you go.

3 Once all the oil has been incorporated, you can adjust the seasoning and also the consistency of the mayo with a little more of the warm water.

4 Store in an airtight container in the fridge for up to 1 week.

5 The mayo will thicken in the fridge, but you can adjust the consistency again by whisking a little water into it.

SRIRACHA MAYO

This mayo *(see Fig. 42)* is part of our second most popular burger, the hot and spicy burger. It is also great for dipping chips into.

MAKES ABOUT 750 G (1 LB 11 OZ/3 CUPS)

1 quantity basic mayo
(see left)

150 ml (5 fl oz) sriracha
chilli sauce

INSTRUCTIONS

1 Mix the ingredients together until well combined. You can always add more or less of the chilli sauce, according to your taste.

2 Keep in an airtight container in the fridge for up to 2 weeks.

SESAME & YUZU MAYO

This nutty, citrusy mayo is found on our organic tofu burger.

MAKES ABOUT 750 G (1 LB 11 OZ/3 CUPS)

80 g (2¾ oz/½ cup) toasted
sesame seeds
1 quantity basic mayo (see left)
40 ml (1¼ fl oz) soy sauce

40 ml (1¼ fl oz) yuzu
juice (if unavailable,
use a mix of lemon
and mandarin juice)

INSTRUCTIONS

1 In a food processor or blender, blitz the sesame seeds for 5–10 seconds to make a fine powder. Don't blitz the seeds for too long, or they will heat up and the oil will come out and make them clumpy.

2 Transfer the sesame powder to a bowl, then add the remaining ingredients and whisk until combined.

3 Keep in an airtight container in the fridge for up to 2 weeks.

MAYONNAISE ^{MN}

GREEN PEPPERCORN MAYO

This one is great with anything meaty –
especially the douche burger on page 90,
with wagyu beef and foie gras!

MAKES ABOUT 750 G (1 LB 11 OZ/3 CUPS)

50 g (1¾ oz/½ cup) green
   peppercorns, fresh if
   possible, otherwise brined
1 quantity basic mayo
   (page 120)

INSTRUCTIONS

1 Blitz the peppercorns in a food processor,
   then mix them through the mayo.

2 Keep in an airtight container in the fridge
   for up to 2 weeks.

JALAPEÑO & THAI BASIL MAYO

The lovely anise flavour of Thai basil
and the subtle kick of fresh jalapeño
chillies makes this mayo *(see Fig. 42)*
a winner with any type of seafood.

MAKES ABOUT 750 G (1 LB 11 OZ/3 CUPS)

1 quantity basic mayo
   (page 120)
2 jalapeño chillies,
   seeds removed

½ bunch (50 g/1¾ oz) Thai
   basil, leaves picked
pinch of citric acid

INSTRUCTIONS

1 Place all the ingredients in a food processor
   and whiz to a purée. Pass through a sieve,
   then place in an airtight container.

2 This mayo will keep in the fridge for up to 2 weeks.

WASABI & MISO MAYO

This is a great dressing for just about any type of seafood *(see Fig 42)*. If you can, try to get nama wasabi, which is a wasabi paste made from real grated wasabi, rather than a powder or paste made with artificial colour and flavour.

MAKES ABOUT 1 KG (2 LB 3 OZ/4 CUPS)

1 quantity basic mayo
   (page 120)
3 tablespoons nama wasabi,
   or wasabi paste if you
   have to

3 tablespoons shiro miso
   (white miso paste)
2 tablespoons light soy sauce
2 tablespoons mirin

INSTRUCTIONS

1 Mix all the ingredients together. Keep in an airtight container in the fridge for up to 1 month.

TONKATSU MAYO

I am a big fan of Japanese crumbed pork, and the tonkatsu sauce that goes with it. It's almost like a Japanese barbecue sauce that has apple and pear blended through it – not unlike a slightly sweeter HP sauce. Tonkatsu sauce is also great in a mayo.

MAKES ABOUT 1 KG (2 LB 3 OZ/4 CUPS)

1 quantity basic mayo
   (page 120)
300 ml (10 fl oz)
   tonkatsu sauce

INSTRUCTIONS

1 Mix the ingredients together and keep in an airtight container in the fridge for up to 1 month.

MAYONNAISE ^{MN}

CRANBERRY MAYO

Turkey goes hand in hand with cranberry sauce! This mayo obviously goes well with the turkey burger on page 64, but is great with just about any poultry, hot or cold *(see Fig. 42)*.

MAKES ABOUT 1 KG (2 LB 3 OZ/4 CUPS)

1 quantity basic mayo
   (page 120)
280 g (10 oz/1 cup)
   cranberry sauce

pinch of sea salt

INSTRUCTIONS

1 Mix the ingredients together and keep in an airtight container in the fridge for up to 1 month.

CHIPOTLE MAYO

Chipotle chillies are smoked and dried jalapeño peppers. They do have a bit of heat, but also a lovely smoky flavour. What we're using here is puréed and strained chipotle chillies in adobo sauce – basically dried chipotle chillies stewed in a sauce of tomato, garlic, vinegar, salt, cumin, oregano and sugar. It is usually sold in tins *(see Fig. 42)*.

MAKES ABOUT 1 KG (2 LB 3 OZ/4 CUPS)

1 quantity basic mayo
   (page 120)
4 tablespoons chipotle chillies
   in adobo sauce, blitzed and
   strained to remove the seeds

1 tablespoon lime juice

INSTRUCTIONS

1 Mix the ingredients together and keep in an airtight container in the fridge for up to 1 month.

BLOODY MARY MAYO

When deciding what to put on our breakfast burger (see page 42), bloody mary mayo *(see Fig. 42)* was a no brainer! The Tabasco and worcestershire sauce go perfectly with egg, and the mustard and horseradish add a spicy freshness.

MAKES ABOUT 750 G (1 LB 11 OZ/3 CUPS)

1 quantity basic mayo
  (page 120)
1 tablespoon Tabasco sauce
1 tablespoon worcestershire
  sauce

1 tablespoon horseradish sauce
1 tablespoon wholegrain
  mustard
1 tablespoon lemon juice
2 tablespoons tomato juice

INSTRUCTIONS

1 Mix all the ingredients together. Keep in an airtight container in the fridge for up to 2 weeks.

THOUSAND ISLAND DRESSING

Growing up in the 1980s, this dressing *(see Fig. 42)* was a bit of a favourite. Having said that, a Reuben (see page 88) is not a Reuben without it. I say the more thousand island dressing the better.

MAKES ABOUT 1 KG (2 LB 3 OZ/4 CUPS)

1 quantity basic mayo
  (page 120)
60 ml (2 fl oz/¼ cup)
  tomato sauce (ketchup)
2 tablespoons finely diced
  gherkins (pickles)
2 French shallots, finely diced

1 tablespoon worcestershire
  sauce
1 teaspoon mustard powder
1 hard-boiled egg, pushed
  through a sieve

INSTRUCTIONS

1 Mix all the ingredients together. Keep in an airtight container in the fridge for up to 2 weeks.

MAYONNAISE ^{MN}

TARTARE SAUCE

I love tartare sauce – it is so delicious with fish and seafood in general. I like it to be quite chunky, so you get the bite of the gherkins, shallots and capers against the richness of the mayonnaise *(see Fig. 42)*.

MAKES ABOUT 1 KG (2 LB 3 OZ/4 CUPS)

1 quantity basic mayo
  (page 120)
45 g (1½ oz/¼ cup) gherkins
  (pickles), finely diced, plus
  2 tablespoons of the gherkin
  pickling juice
45 g (1½ oz/¼ cup) capers,
  finely chopped

4 French shallots, finely diced
2 hard-boiled eggs, pushed
  through a sieve
3 tablespoons flat-leaf (Italian)
  parsley, thinly sliced

INSTRUCTIONS

1 Mix all the ingredients together. Keep in an airtight container in the fridge for up to 2 weeks.

LEMON AÏOLI

This is an absolute classic and goes very well with all seafood, especially calamari. Don't be afraid of garlic, it's your friend, and also good for you.

MAKES ABOUT 750 G (1 LB 11 OZ/3 CUPS)

1 quantity basic mayo
  (page 120)
4 garlic cloves, crushed
juice of 2 lemons

½ teaspoon freshly ground
  black pepper

INSTRUCTIONS

1 Mix all the ingredients together. Keep in an airtight container in the fridge for up to 2 weeks.

2 The flavour will get stronger the longer you leave it.

ONION & MUSTARD JAM ^{OM}

This is really more of a relish than a jam *(see Fig. 43)*. It is slightly sweet, but the bite of the mustard balances it well. This goes well on cold meats too.

MAKES ABOUT 300 G (10½ OZ/1 CUP)

2 tablespoons vegetable oil
2 tablespoons brown
   mustard seeds
4 onions, thinly sliced
4 garlic cloves, crushed
330 ml (11 fl oz) dark beer

125 ml (4 fl oz/½ cup)
   malt vinegar
90 g (3 oz) brown sugar
1 tablespoon mustard powder
1 bay leaf

INSTRUCTIONS

1 Heat a non-stick saucepan over a medium heat and add the oil. Add the mustard seeds and let them pop for a moment, then add the onion and garlic. Sprinkle the onions and garlic with a couple of pinches of salt and freshly ground black pepper.

2 Cook, stirring frequently, for about 5 minutes, or until the onion starts to soften. Add the remaining ingredients and simmer over a low heat for about 20 minutes, until the mixture starts to thicken.

3 Remove the bay leaf, season to taste, then place in an airtight container to cool.

4 Store in the fridge for up to 1 month.

CARAMELISED ONION ^{CO}

Onions have a lot of sugar in them and when cooked slowly, they caramelise and become very sweet *(see Fig. 43)*. They go beautifully with just about any meat.

MAKES ABOUT 275 G (9½ OZ/1 CUP)

30 g (1 oz) butter
2 large brown onions,
   thinly sliced

50 ml (1¾ fl oz)
   balsamic vinegar

INSTRUCTIONS

1 Heat a saucepan over a medium heat and add the butter. Once the butter has melted and is sizzling slightly, add the onion and a little salt and freshly ground black pepper.

2 Turn the heat down to low and cook for about 20 minutes, stirring frequently, until the onion has turned golden and caramelised.

3 Stir in the vinegar and cook for a further 5–10 minutes, until the mixture has reduced and thickened.

4 Check the seasoning and place in an airtight container. Store in the fridge for up to 1 month.

SRIRACHA

MISO

TARTARE

BLOODY MARY

— Fig. 42 —

CHIPOTLE

THOUSAND ISLAND

CRANBERRY

JALAPENO

— Fig. 42 —

TOMATO KASUNDI ^{KS}

This Indian relish *(see Fig. 43)* is delicious with just about all red meats, fish, chicken and vegetables. It is relatively easy to make and will keep for a couple of months in a clean container in the fridge.

MAKES ABOUT 500 G (1 LB 2 OZ/2 CUPS)

1 tablespoon brown
  mustard seeds
125 ml (4 fl oz/½ cup)
  cider vinegar
2 kg (4 lb 6 oz) tomatoes
10 bird's eye chillies
125 ml (4 fl oz/½ cup)
  vegetable oil
10 garlic cloves, crushed
2 teaspoons finely grated
  fresh ginger

1 tablespoon very finely
  chopped fresh turmeric,
  or 1 tablespoon ground
  turmeric
pinch of ground cloves
2 tablespoons cumin seeds,
  lightly toasted and ground
60 ml (2 fl oz/¼ cup)
  fish sauce
75 g (2¾ oz) palm
  sugar (jaggery), chopped

INSTRUCTIONS

1 Preheat the oven to 180°C (350°F).

2 Place the mustard seeds in a small saucepan with the vinegar and simmer over a low heat for 10 minutes, or until all the vinegar is absorbed.

3 Cut the 'eyes' out of the tomatoes, and the stalks off the chillies. Toss the tomatoes and chillies with a tablespoon of the oil and place in a baking dish. Roast for 15–20 minutes, or until the tomato skins split. Leave to cool slightly, then work the tomatoes and chillies through a mouli, or force them through a large-holed conical strainer.

4 Blend the garlic, ginger, turmeric, cloves and cumin in a food processor or blender until smooth.

5 Heat the remaining oil in a wide-based saucepan. Fry off the spice paste for 5 minutes, or until fragrant. Stir in the tomato and chilli mixture and the vinegary mustard seeds. Simmer for about 30 minutes, or until thick.

6 Stir in the fish sauce and palm sugar and simmer for a further 5 minutes.

7 Transfer from the pan into a suitable container to cool, then store in an airtight container in the fridge for up to 2 months.

TOMATO & QUINCE RELISH ^{TQ}

This is a seasonal variation on regular tomato sauce. The sweetness and flavour of the quince goes really well with the maple-glazed bacon hot dog recipe on page 85, and also gives a lovely consistency.

MAKES ABOUT 400 G (14 OZ/1½ CUPS)

250 g (9 oz) caster (superfine) sugar
1 star anise
½ cinnamon stick
1 cardamom pod, cracked
1 quince
2 tomatoes, peeled, seeded and diced

2 French shallots, very finely diced
4 garlic cloves, sliced
150 ml (5 fl oz) malt vinegar
2 tablespoons tomato paste (concentrated purée)

INSTRUCTIONS

1 Place the sugar, spices and 500 ml (17 fl oz/ 2 cups) water in a saucepan and bring to the boil. Meanwhile, peel the quince, cut into quarters and cut away the core.

2 Reduce the heat to low and add the quince to the syrup. Cover with a round of baking paper and cook gently for 30 minutes, or until soft. Remove from the heat and set side to cool.

3 Pour 200 ml (7 fl oz) of the quince poaching syrup into a clean saucepan, discarding the spices. Dice the quince and add to the pan, along with all the remaining ingredients. Stir to combine, then bring to the boil. Reduce the heat to a simmer and cook for a further 15 minutes, or until the mixture is soft and slightly thickened. Season to taste with sea salt and freshly ground black pepper.

4 Set aside to cool slightly. Transfer the mixture to a blender, purée to a smooth sauce, then transfer to a clean bottle. Store in the fridge for up to 1 month.

BACON SALT ^{BS}

Sprinkle liberally over any food to add
a delicious bacon flavour *(see Fig. 43)*.

MAKES ABOUT 3 TABLESPOONS

8 bacon rashers (slices)
2 tablespoons salt

INSTRUCTIONS

1 Preheat the oven to its lowest setting.

2 Heat a non-stick grill pan over a medium heat
and cook the bacon until it is crisp. Immediately
drain on paper towel and place another paper
towel on top. Press lightly to extract as much
grease as possible.

3 Spread the bacon in a single layer between
clean sheets of paper towel, on a large baking
tray. Dry out in the oven for 6 hours.

4 Place the bacon in a food processor with the salt
and pulse until fine. Store in an airtight container
at room temperature – do not put in the fridge.
The bacon salt will keep for up to 2 weeks.

BEETROOT ^{BT}

The sharpness and sweetness of beetroot is a perfect complement to charred meat and other salad components. Please do try to make your own pickled beetroot at home, as it's so much better than the tinned stuff and really quite simple.

MAKES ABOUT 400 G (14 OZ/2 CUPS)

3 large beetroot (beets), washed well
125 ml (4 fl oz/½ cup) white vinegar
115 g (4 oz/½ cup) caster (superfine) sugar
3 tablespoons sea salt
2 bay leaves
2 tablespoons black peppercorns
2 star anise
1 cinnamon stick

INSTRUCTIONS

1 Place the beetroot in a large saucepan and cover with water to 5 cm (2 in) above the top of the beetroot. Add the remaining ingredients and bring to a simmer.

2 Simmer over a medium heat for about 30 minutes, or until the beetroot are soft when pierced with a small knife. Allow to cool slightly in the liquid for maximum moistness and flavour.

3 Once cool enough to handle, drain the beetroot in a colander. Put on some disposable gloves to protect your hands from staining red, then gently use your thumbs to slip the skins off. The skins should come off quite easily, provided the beetroot are not completely cold. (Don't place them in the fridge prior to peeling as this will make the skin stick.)

4 Slice the beetroot to your desired thickness and reserve in an airtight container in the fridge until ready to use. The beetroot will keep in the fridge for up to 3 months.

BACON SALT

ONION & MUSTARD JAM

— Fig. 43 —

TOMATO
KASUNDI

PICKLES

CARAMELISED ONION

— Fig. 43 —

PICKLES ^{PK}

Pickles in a burger help balance out the rich fattiness of beef. These pickles *(see Fig. 43)* are nice to have in the fridge for other uses, such as tossing through a potato salad or even tartare sauce.

MAKES ABOUT 1 KG (2 LB 3 OZ)

4 x 250 g (9 oz) punnets
   baby cucumbers, *or* 4 large
   Lebanese (short) cucumbers

Pickling spice mix
1 teaspoon freshly ground
   black pepper
1 teaspoon mustard seeds
1 teaspoon coriander seeds
½ teaspoon chilli flakes
½ teaspoon allspice berries
½ teaspoon mace
pinch of ground cinnamon
8 bay leaves
pinch of cloves
large pinch of ground ginger

Brine
65 g (2¼ oz/½ cup) salt
125 ml (4 fl oz/½ cup)
   white vinegar
½ teaspoon black peppercorns
2 teaspoons pickling spice

INSTRUCTIONS

1 For the pickling spice mix, put all the spices together in a dry frying pan and toast over a medium heat for a few minutes, until fragrant. Using a food processor or spice grinder, pulse into a fine powder.

2 For the brine, combine all the ingredients in a large saucepan. Add the powdered spice mix and 1.25 litres (42 fl oz/5 cups) water and bring to the boil. Leave to bubble away for 3 minutes, then remove from the heat. Strain through a fine sieve and allow to cool.

3 Slice the cucumbers 2–3 mm (⅛ in) thick, using a mandoline or a sharp knife. Place the slices in the cold brine and submerge with an upside-down plate. Leave to pickle in the fridge for at least 24 hours.

4 Store the cucumbers in the brine in an airtight container. The pickles will keep in the fridge for up to 3 months.

CUCUMBER & SHALLOT PICKLE ^{CS}

This is a very simple and quick pickle. It is great for cutting through the fattiness and richness of the maple-glazed bacon hot dog recipe on page 85.

MAKES ABOUT 280 G (10 OZ/1 CUP)

1 telegraph (long) cucumber, peeled, seeded and coarsely grated

2 French shallots, very finely diced

150 ml (5 fl oz) chardonnay vinegar

55 g (2 oz/¼ cup) caster (superfine) sugar

1 teaspoon brown mustard seeds

½ teaspoon dill seeds

1 teaspoon chopped dill

INSTRUCTIONS

1 Place all the ingredients, except the chopped dill, into a saucepan over a medium heat. Stir to combine, then cook for 4 minutes, or until the mixture thickens slightly and resembles a relish.

2 Set aside to cool, then stir the dill through. This pickle is best used fresh, but will keep in an airtight container in the fridge for up to 1 week.

ACKNOWLEDGEMENTS

First and foremost I would like to thank all of the staff who have worked in our stores and shared our vision to bring our burgers to the people.

The amazing team assembled by Hardie Grant have again made a beautiful book. Suzy and Cassie from A Friend of Mine knocked it out of the park with the design, so much fun! Deb Kaloper, you made me want to eat each page with your perfect styling. Chris Middleton, you know how to make my buns look their best through the lens! Hannah Koelmeyer, thanks for guiding me through the process and keeping me on track with a gentle hand. Katri Hilden, thanks for picking up all my mistakes and making me look smarter with your editing. Mark Campbell, thanks for popping in and taking care of the leftover kale! A big thanks to Aileen and Stephen Lord for allowing us to take over your place (again) for the shoot. Roxy Ryan and Caitlin Neville, thanks in advance for getting the word out there about this book and making it a huge success. Finally Paul McNally and the entire Hardie Grant team, who believe in books like this and work hard behind the scenes: *THANKS!*

On a personal level this is not possible without the unwavering support from my beautiful wife and daughters Leah, Grace and Maddie. You all build me up day to day and give me belief in these sometimes crazy ideas. I love you all very much. To Mum, Dad, Ade, Aunty Prit, Eddie and Loretta: though we may be far apart, your love and support is always felt and appreciated. Big love back to you all.

Dante and Jeff, we share these crazy ideas with each other and egg each other on to make it happen. So far so good, and let's keep it going for a long time. Our combined youthful enthusiasm and tenacity is a rare find, I think, and I am glad to be partners with you two. Rachel and Katie you also must have the patience of saints to go along with our madness!

Jerome, Neil and the other suppliers have been there to underpin the quality of the food, and without you we could not be where we are.

A

aïoli
Lemon aïoli **126**

American (processed)
cheese **22**
American yellow mustard **20**

apple
Fennel & apple slaw **62**

arugula (rocket) **30**

B

bacon
Bacon & egg burger **42**
Bacon maple milkshake
syrup **18, 107**
Bacon salt **132**
Bacon sausages **85**
Double cheeseburger with
bacon **46, 115**
Kassler (Canadian) **18**
Maple-glazed bacon dog
with tomato & quince
relish & mustard pickles
85
streaky or middle **18**
Works burger **40**

Baked macaroni with
three cheeses **102**
Barbecue sauce **94, 115**
Basic mayo **120**
Basic milkshake syrup **105**
Béchamel sauce **102**
beef *see* corned beef;
wagyu beef
beer, choosing **92–3**
beer batter **100**

beetroot **32**
pickling recipe **133**
Bintje potatoes **26**
Bloody Mary mayo **125**

Blue cheese **22**
breakfast burger **42**
Brined pickles **28**

buns
brioche **10**
sesame seed **10**
soft burger **114**
toasting inside **10, 12**
wholemeal/wholegrain **10**

burger patty **14–15**

burger patty, meat for
cuts **15**
fat content **14, 15**
grass-fed or grain-fed **14**
grinding **15**
marbling **14**
seasoning **15**
shrinkage **13**
terroir **14**
wagyu **14, 36**

butter, clarified **12, 117**
butter lettuce **30**

C

caramel *see* salt – salted
caramel syrup

caramelisation **94**
Caramelised onion **127**

chargrilling **15**

cheese
American (processed) **22**
Baked macaroni with
three cheeses **102**
Béchamel sauce **102**
Blue **22**
Cheddar **22**
Double cheeseburger
with bacon **46**
Gruyère & mustard
sauce **85**

Mozzarella **22**
Pepper Jack **22**
Swiss **22**
The Works Burger **40**
Wagyu cheeseburger
deluxe **36**

Cherry ketchup **116**

chicken & turkey
Fried chicken burger **48**
Honey soy chicken burger
with sesame slaw **66**
Karaage chicken burger
with wombok slaw
& pickled ginger
mayo **68**
Turkey burger with cranberry
mayo & kale **64**

Chickpea burger with tahini
yoghurt **74**

chilli
Chilli dressing **78**
Jalapeño & Thai basil
mayo **122**

Chipotle mayo **124**

chips
crinkle-cut **27**
French fries **27**
'hand-cut' **26, 27, 98**
making **26, 98**
potatoes for **26, 98**
shoestring **27**
straight-cut **27**
wedges **27**
see also potatoes – crisps

Chocolate honeycomb
milkshake syrup **108**
Chocolate milkshake syrup **107**
Clam po' burger boy
with jalapeño & Thai
basil mayo **80**
Clarified butter **12, 117**
Classic hot dog **84**
Coliban potatoes **26**

corned beef
The Reuben burger **88**

Cornichons **28**
cos lettuce **30**

crab
cleaning **78**
Soft-shell crab burger
with green mango salad
& chilli dressing **78**

Cranberry mayo **124**
Crinkle-cut chips **27**

crumbing
Crumbed snapper burger
with tartare sauce **70**
Tonkatsu pork with apple
& fennel slaw **62**

cucumber
Cucumber & shallot
pickle **137**
Pickled cucumber **52**
Pickles **136**

D

Dijon mustard **20**
Dill (kosher) pickles **28**
Double cheeseburger
with bacon **46**
Douche burger **90, 122**

dressings
Chilli **78**
'dijonnaise' **20**
Thousand island **125**

E

eggs
Bacon & egg burger **42**
fried **32**
for mayo **120**

F

Fennel & apple slaw **62**

fish & seafood burgers
Clam po' boy burger
with jalapeño & Thai
basil mayo **80**
Crumbed snapper burger
with tartare sauce **70**
Lobster burger with tobiko
& wasabi & miso
mayo **75**
Prawn togarashi burger with
yuzu & sesame mayo **76**
see also crab

flour, spiced **48**, **80**
focaccia **10**
French fries **27**
Fried chicken burger **48**

G

ghee **117**
gherkins **28**

ginger
Pickled ginger mayo **68**

grain- or grass-fed beef **14**
Green mango salad **78**
Green peppercorn mayo **122**
Grilled ham & pineapple burger
with chipotle mayo **60**
Gruyère & mustard sauce **85**

H

Half-sized burger **38**

ham
Grilled ham & pineapple
burger with chipotle
mayo **60**

Hand-cut chips **26**, **27**, **98**

Hawaiian burger **32**
Grilled ham & pineapple
burger with chipotle
mayo **60**

Honey mustard **20**
Honey soy chicken burger
with sesame slaw **66**

Honeycomb **108**
Chocolate honeycomb
syrup **108**

Horseradish cream **86**
Hot & spicy deluxe burger **47**

hot dogs
Classic hot dog **84**
Maple-glazed bacon dog
with tomato & quince
relish & mustard pickles
85, **131**

Hot English mustard **20**
How to eat a burger **54–5**

J

Jalapeño mayo **48**
Jalapeño & Thai basil
mayo **122**

K

Kaiserfleisch (streaky) bacon **18**
kale **30**
Karaage chicken burger
with wombok slaw & pickled
ginger mayo **68**
Kassler (Canadian) bacon **18**
Kennebec potatoes **26**

ketchup
Cherry ketchup **116**
origins **20**
Tomato ketchup **116**

L

Lamb burger with mint yoghurt
and pickled cucumber **56**
leafy greens **30**
Lemon aïoli **126**

lettuce
as burger wrap **30**
butter (bibb) **30**
cos (romaine) **30**
iceberg **30**
washing **30**

Lobster burger with tobikko
& wasabe & miso mayo **75**

M

Maple-glazed bacon dog
with tomato & quince relish
and mustard pickles **85**

mayonnaise **120**
Basic mayo **120**
Bloody Mary mayo **125**
Chipotle mayo **124**
Cranberry mayo **124**
Green peppercorn
mayo **122**
Jalapeño mayo **48**
Jalapeño & Thai basil
mayo **122**
Lemon aïoli **126**
Pickled ginger mayo **68**
Sesame & yuzu mayo **121**
Sriracha mayo **121**
Tartare sauce **126**
Thousand Island
dressing **125**
Tonkatsu mayo **123**
Wasabi & miso mayo **123**

middle bacon **18**

milkshake syrups
Bacon maple **18**, **107**
Basic milkshake **105**
Chocolate **107**
Chocolate honeycomb **108**
Peanut butter **106**
Salted caramel **109**
Strawberry **105**
Vanilla **106**

Mint yoghurt **52**

miso
Wasabi & miso mayo **123**

Mozzarella **22**

mustard
American **20**
commercial **20**
dijon **20**
Gruyère & mustard sauce
85
Honey **20**
Hot English **20**
Onion & mustard jam **127**
Spicy **117**
Wholegrain or 'seed' **20**

O

onion
Caramelised onion **127**
Onion & mustard jam **127**
Onion rings **100**

Organic tofu burger **50**, **121**

P

pasta
Baked macaroni with
three cheeses **102**

Peanut butter milkshake
syrup **106**
Pepper Jack cheese **22**

Peppered steak burger
with caramelised onion
& horseradish cream **86**

pickles **136**
battered & deep-fried **28**
Beetroot **133**
Brined pickles **28**
Cornichons **28**
Cucumber & shallot **137**
Cucumbers **136**
Dill (kosher) **28**
Gherkins **28**
inside or on the side **28**
making your own **136**
meaning **28**
Pickled cucumber **52**
Pickled ginger mayo **68**
spice mix **136**

pide (Turkish bread) **10**

pineapple
fresh **32**
Grilled ham & pineapple
burger with chipotle
mayo **60**
grilling **32**
Works burger **40**

pommes frites **27**

pork
Smoked pulled-pork burger
with pickles **58**
Tonkatsu pork with apple
& fennel slaw **62**

potatoes
crisps **26, 104**
wedges **27**
see also chips

Prawn togarashi burger with
yuzu & sesame mayo **76**

Q

quince
Tomato & quince relish **131**

R

relish
Onion & mustard jam **127**
Tomato & quince relish **131**
Tomato kasundi **130**

The Reuben burger **22, 88, 89**
rocket (arugula) **30**
Russet burbank
potatoes **26, 98**

S

salads
Green mango salad **78**
leafy greens **30**
see also slaw

salt
Bacon salt **132**
Salted caramel milkshake
syrup **108**
Salted caramel syrup **109**

sauces
Barbecue sauce **94, 115**
Béchamel sauce **102**
Gruyère & mustard sauce **85**
see also ketchup

sauerkraut
The Reuben burger
22, 88, 89

sausages
Bacon sausages **85**

seafood *see* fish & seafood
burgers
seasoning **15**
Sebago potatoes **26**

seed (wholegrain) mustard **20**
Sesame & yuzu mayo **121**
Sesame seed bun **10**
Sesame slaw **66**

shallots
Cucumber & shallot
pickle **137**

shoestring chips **27**

Slaw **48**
Fennel & apple slaw **62**
Sesame slaw **66**
Wombok slaw **68**

Smoked pulled-pork burger
with pickles **58**
Soft burger buns **114**
Soft-shell crab burger
with green mango salad
& chilli dressing **78**
Spiced flour **48, 80**
Spicy mustard **117**
Sriracha mayo **121**
Straight-cut chips **27**
Strawberry milkshake
syrup **105**
Swiss cheese **22**
syrups for milkshakes
see milkshake syrups

T

Tahini yoghurt **74**
Tartare sauce **126**

Thai-style burger
Soft-shell crab burger
with green mango salad
& chilli dressing **78–9**

tofu
Organic tofu burger
50, 121

tomato
slices **32**
Tomato & quince relish **131**
Tomato kasundi **130**
Tomato ketchup **116**

Tonkatsu mayo **123**
Tonkatsu pork with apple
& fennel slaw **62**
Turkey burger with cranberry
mayo & kale **64**

V

Vanilla milkshake syrup **106**

vegetarian burgers
Chickpea burger with
tahini yoghurt **72, 74**
Organic tofu burger
50, 121

W

wagyu beef
marbling **14**

Wagyu cheeseburger deluxe
36
Wasabi & miso mayo **123**
'which beer?' project **92–5**
wholegrain ('seed') mustard **20**
Wombok slaw **68**
Works burger **40**

Y

yoghurt
Mint yoghurt **52**
Tahini yoghurt **74**

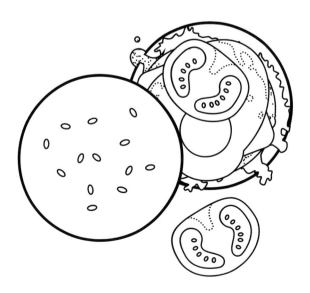

**FIRST PUBLISHED IN 2015 BY HARDIE GRANT BOOKS,
AN IMPRINT OF HARDIE GRANT PUBLISHING**

THIS EDITION PUBLISHED IN 2017

HARDIE GRANT BOOKS (MELBOURNE)
Building 1, 658 Church Street
Richmond, Victoria 3121
www.hardiegrantbooks.com.au

HARDIE GRANT BOOKS (LONDON)
5th & 6th Floors
52–54 Southwark Street
London SE1 1UN
www.hardiegrantbooks.co.uk

A Cataloguing-in-Publication entry is available
from the catalogue of the National Library
of Australia at www.nla.gov.au

Burger Lab
ISBN 978 1 74379 275 9

PUBLISHING DIRECTOR: Paul McNally
PROJECT EDITOR: Hannah Koelmeyer
EDITOR: Katri Hilden
DESIGN MANAGER: Mark Campbell
DESIGN & ART DIRECTION: A Friend of Mine
ILLUSTRATION: Cassie Brock at A Friend of Mine
PHOTOGRAPHER: Chris Middleton
STYLIST: Deb Kaloper
PRODUCTION MANAGER: Todd Rechner

Special thanks to K.W.Doggett Fine Paper for
supplying all of the beautiful coloured backgrounds.

Colour reproduction by Splitting Image Colour Studio
Printed in China by 1010 Printing International
Limited